Nichola Boughey • Steve Day
Colette Roberts • Sarah Webb

Series editors: Martin Collier • Rosemary Rees

Book 2

Cover image: A preliminary study for 'Work' by Ford Madox Brown from 1863 (oil on canvas). This scene was designed to show all aspects of Victorian society. (c) Manchester Art Gallery, UK/ The Bridgeman Art Library.

www.heinemann.co.uk

✓ Free online support
✓ Useful weblinks
✓ 24 hour online ordering

01865 888080

Heinemann is an imprint of Pearson Education Limited, a company incorporated in England and Wales, having its registered office at Edinburgh Gate, Harlow, Essex, CM20 2JE. Registered company number: 872828

www.heinemann.co.uk

Heinemann is a registered trademark of Pearson Education Limited

Text © Pearson Education Limited 2008

First published 2008

12

10 9 8 7

British Library Cataloguing in Publication Data is available from the British Library on request.
ISBN 978 0 435318 94 9

Freelance edited by Sandra Stafford

Designed and typeset by Ian Lansley

Original illustrations © Pearson Education Ltd 2008

Illustrated by NB Illusration and Tek-Art, Crawley Down, West Sussex

Cover design by David Poole

Picture research by Ned Coomes

Cover photo/illustration © Birmingham Museums and Art Gallery

Printed in China (CTPS/07)

The author and publisher would like to thank the following individuals and organisation for permission to reproduce photographs:

akg-images: 7e; Amoret Tanner/Alamy: 113b; Andrew Holt/National Maritime Museum, London: 72a; Archives Charmet/Bridgeman Art Library: 74a; ARPL/HIP/TopFoto: 75d; Bettmann/Corbis UK Ltd: 85h, 171e; Bibliotheque des Arts Decoratifs, Paris, France/Archives Charmet/Bridgeman Art Library: 170a; Birmingham Museums and Art Gallery/Bridgeman Art Library: 20a; Bridgeman Art Library: 10a, 13b. 21g, 28a, 40d, 124a, 124d, 6b, 60b; Bristol City Museum and Art Gallery, UK/Bridgeman Art Library: 142a; British Library/akg-images: 21h; British Museum, London, UK/Bridgeman Art Library: 49e; Claudet/Getty Images: 122a; Corbis UK Ltd: 80a, 104a, 139h, 150; Courtesy of the Council, National Army Museum, London, UK/Bridgeman Art Library: 172a; Courtesy of the Trustees of Sir John Soane's Museum, London/Bridgeman Art Library: 52a; David Hoffman Photo Library/Alamy: 42a; David Robertson/Alamy: 160a; Fotomas/TopFoto: 8a, 13c; Gerald Bloncourt RA/Lebrecht Music and Arts: 40a; Gianni Dagli Orti/Corbis UK Ltd: 7e, 36b; HIP/The British Library/TopFoto: 29b; Hulton Archive/Getty Images: 6a, 68, 130c; Hulton-Deutsch Collection/Corbis UK Ltd: 175c; Illustrated London News/Mary Evans Picture Library: 156b; Library of Congress: 56a; Library of Congress, Washington D.C., USA/Bridgeman Art Library: 138c; Liverpool Record Office/Liverpool Record Office: 143e; London Stereoscopic Company/Getty Images: 128r; Lordprice Collection/Alamy: 138b; Manchester Art Gallery, UK/Bridgeman Art Library: 47a; Mansell/Time & Life Pictures/Getty Images: 119d; Mary Evans Picture Library: 13a, 168d; Mary Evans Picture Library/Alamy: 6c, 56b, 68a, 74b, 75c, 102c, 115b, 168b, 171c; Museum of London, UK/Bridgeman Art Library: 70a; Museum of London/HIP /TopFoto: 118c; National Archives: 7d, 123b; National Maritime Museum, London, UK/Bridgeman Art Library: 176b; Newport Museum and Art Gallery, South Wales/Bridgeman Art Library: 54a; North Wind Picture Archives/Alamy: 88g, 92e, 138a; NRM - Pictorial Collection/Science & Society Picture Library: 116a; Owen Beattie/University of Alberta: 155a; PhotoSpin, Inc/Alamy; 90a; Private Collection/© Royal Exchange Art Gallery at Cork Street, London/Bridgeman Art Library: 162a; Punch Limited/Topham/TopFoto: 104c; Rob Brimson/Taxi/Getty Images: 176a; Roger-Viollet/TopFoto; 39a; © Royal Geographical Society, London, UK/Bridgeman Art Library: 152a; Sir Edmund Verney and the Claydon House Trust/Courtauld Institute of Art: 67a; Stapleton Collection, UK/Bridgeman Art Library: 31c; Stapleton Collection/Corbis UK Ltd: 105d, 119e, 143f; State Archives of Florida: 82a, 86b; Stiftung Maximilianeum, Munchen: 32a; The Drambuie Collection, Edinburgh, Scotland/Bridgeman Art Library: 26a; The Print Collector /Alamy: 22, 102a, 104b, 114a, 118a, 128m, 121f, 138c, 156a; The Trustees of the Goodwood Collection/Bridgeman Art Library: 20b; TopFoto: 15, 168c; Topham Picturepoint/TopFoto: 118b, 140k, 128l; Underwood & Underwood/Corbis UK Ltd: 1484a; Visual Arts Library (London)/Alamy: 138d, 168a; Walker Art Gallery/Bridgeman Art Library: 177d; Wellcome Library, London/Wellcome Trust: 81d; © Wilberforce House, Hull City Museums and Art Galleries, UK/Bridgeman Art Library 144b, 149d; Woolaroc Museum, Oklahoma, USA, Peter Newark Western Americana/Bridgeman Art Library 94a

Every effort has been made to contact copyright holders of material reproduced in this book. Any omissions will be rectified in subsequent printings if notice is given to the publishers.

Websites

There are links to relevant websites in this book. In order to ensure that the links are up to date, that the links work, and that the sites are not inadvertently linked to sites that could be considered offensive, we have made the links available on the Heinemann website at www.heinemann.co.uk/hotlinks. When you access the site, the express code is 8949T.

Contents

Finding out about history

This book has been written to bring your Key Stage 3 History lessons alive and to make sure you get the most out of them! The book is divided into three sections:
Ruling, Living and working and **Moving and travelling**.

By looking at each of these big themes, you will build up a picture of what life was like for people living in the period 1603 to 1901. This was a time of great change. It saw the overthrow of kings and rulers, the birth of the United Kingdom, the development of industry and the growth of empires. You will be able to find out why these changes happened and how they affected the way people lived and worked, moved around, ruled and were ruled.

But this book isn't just about England and later Britain. You'll have a chance to find out about what was happening in other parts of the world and how these events affected Britain. You can also begin to explore how decisions made in Britain might affect people around the globe.

Doing history!

In each section of this book there are activities to help you get the most out of that topic. Most sections will have four different types of task, though some will just have the first three:

1 Everyone should be able to have a go at this task.

2 Next, have a go at this task.

3 Once you've completed the blue task, see if you can try this.

4 If you want to stretch yourself, you can have a go at this.

History detective
There will be chances for you to investigate topics in more detail and carry out your own investigations.

Back to the start
You will also be able to review and reflect on the bigger picture and on your own learning.

Practising historical skills

At the end of the book, you'll find a Skills bank. This is to remind you of some of the important historical skills you'll be learning. Use this section for useful hints and tips as you complete the tasks and the activities throughout the book.

Introduction

Between 1603 and 1901 there were big changes in who held power in England and in different countries around the world. In England, the monarch held power in 1603, but by 1901 power was firmly in the hands of Parliament.

Members of Parliament are elected by the people to make laws. At the beginning of the period only a few wealthy men were allowed to vote, but by the end of the period the number of people who could vote had greatly increased. These changes in who held power sometimes came about peacefully. At other times change came through the use of violence.

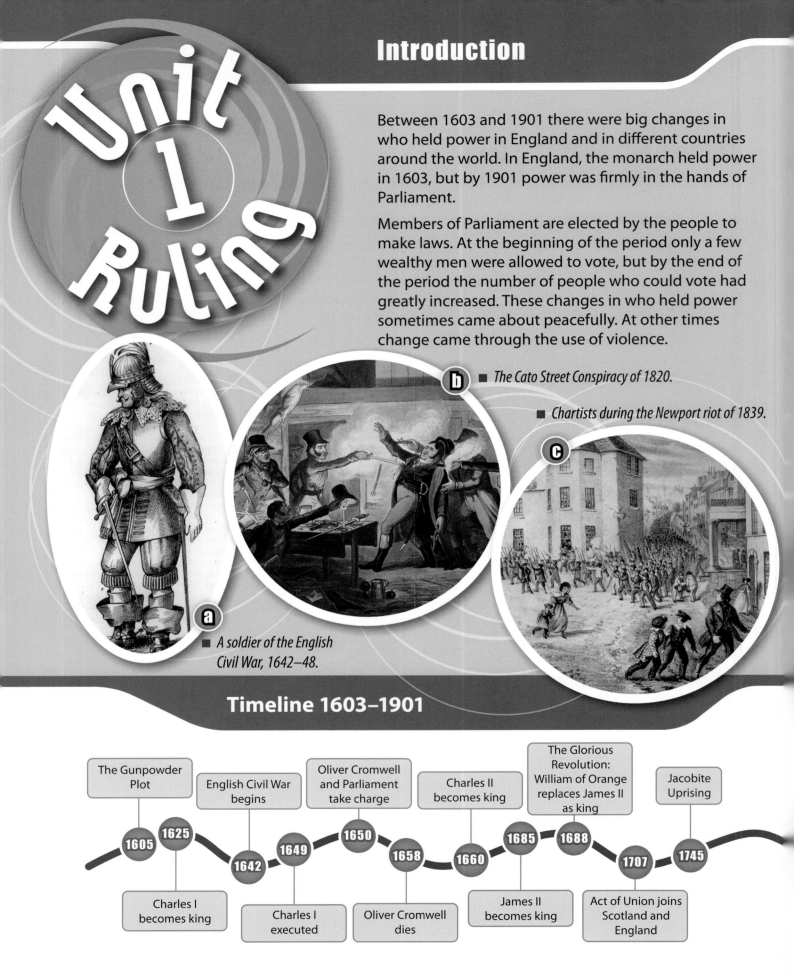

- *The Cato Street Conspiracy of 1820.*

- *Chartists during the Newport riot of 1839.*

- *A soldier of the English Civil War, 1642–48.*

Timeline 1603–1901

| The Gunpowder Plot | English Civil War begins | Oliver Cromwell and Parliament take charge | Charles II becomes king | The Glorious Revolution: William of Orange replaces James II as king | Jacobite Uprising |

1605 · 1625 · 1642 · 1649 · 1650 · 1658 · 1660 · 1685 · 1688 · 1707 · 1745

| Charles I becomes king | Charles I executed | Oliver Cromwell dies | James II becomes king | Act of Union joins Scotland and England |

Each picture (a–e) shows some of the ways in which people tried to change who held power between 1603 and 1901.

1 With a partner, identify the methods people are using to challenge those in power in each picture. Think carefully about whether the methods are violent or peaceful.

2 Why do you think attempts to change who held power so often resulted in violence? In your pairs try to suggest at least two reasons.

3 Use the timeline to identify other ways in which people tried to challenge those in power.

4 Use the timeline and the information on these pages to identify what you think were the main changes that took place in who held power during the period 1603 to 1901.

■ *Women campaigning for the right to vote in 1887.*

■ *Execution of Marie Antoinette in 1793.*

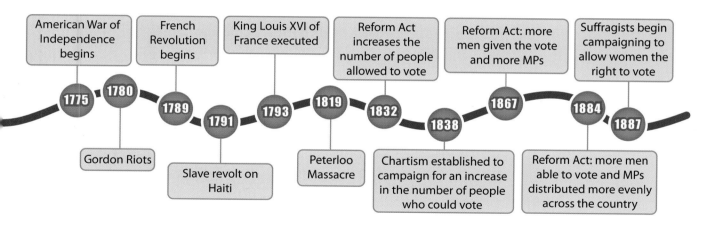

American War of Independence begins — 1775

French Revolution begins — 1789

King Louis XVI of France executed — 1793

Reform Act increases the number of people allowed to vote — 1832

Reform Act: more men given the vote and more MPs — 1867

Suffragists begin campaigning to allow women the right to vote

1780

Gordon Riots

1791 — Slave revolt on Haiti

1819 — Peterloo Massacre

1838 — Chartism established to campaign for an increase in the number of people who could vote

1884 — Reform Act: more men able to vote and MPs distributed more evenly across the country

1887

In this lesson you will:

- find out about the religious and political problems in seventeenth-century England

- weigh up the problems that the king faced.

The world turned upside down

The seventeenth century was a chaotic time for many people and several things were changing in their lives.

? *Look at source a. What can you see that looks peculiar? Do you think the artist actually saw these things? What is the artist trying to show?*

a

THE
World turn'd upfide down:
OR
A briefe defcription of the ridiculous Fafhions of thefe diftracted Times.

By T. J. a well-willer to King, Parliament and Kingdom.

■ *This picture is taken from a pamphlet produced in 1647.*

Get in Character

1 Imagine you are a person from the seventeenth century.

a) First, give yourself a name. Look at the examples below of typical names from this century.

First name		Last name	
Jeremiah	Katherine	Denton	Hutchinson
Hugh	Elizabeth	Croft	Cowley
Richard	Mary	Fanshawe	Harley
Edmund	Anne	Montrose	Littleton

b) Now choose the way you earn your living.

farmer	merchant	potter
inn keeper	clothes maker	clothes washer

c) Decide where you will live. It can be your home town, where your school is or somewhere else miles away in Britain!

d) Finally, choose the type of Christian you want to be:

Catholic	Church of England	Puritan

Remember most people in England at this time were Christians, but not everyone belonged to the same church.

Key words

Divine right
This is the idea that someone has been chosen by God to be a ruler.

Jesuit
A type of Catholic priest.

MP or MPs
An abbreviation for Member of Parliament or Members of Parliament.

Think it over

2 Read through the eight speech bubbles below. Decide which your character would be most concerned about and why. Are your concerns the same as your partner's? If not, how are they different?

> My cousin, who lives in London, has told me that a group of Catholics, led by a man called Guy Fawkes, has tried to blow up the Houses of Parliament!

> England used to be a Catholic country and it's not fair to treat us all like traitors. Most of us don't want to overthrow the king and replace him with a Catholic monarch.

> I'm a Puritan, and I'm worried that the Church of England is becoming too similar to the Catholic Church. There are candles and crucifixes everywhere. The king should put a stop to this!

> My Catholic neighbour is very afraid. He says that his family is persecuted for attending church and that he's found it difficult to get a job.

> King James allows his son Charles' Catholic wife, Henrietta Maria, to go to Catholic services at court. I sometimes wonder if he might secretly be a Catholic!

> People are saying that the king is getting too powerful. For example, he's collecting taxes without the permission of Parliament.

> As an **MP**, I have freedom of speech and can discuss decisions that the king has made and give him advice. Trouble is, the king doesn't seem to be listening to us.

> I overheard some **MPs** talking and they say the king thinks he can rule by **divine right**. He says he has the right to call Parliament and to shut it down, and that only he can decide on foreign policy. What's the point of having MPs if the king can behave like that?

 b

> Since the **Jesuits** set foot in this land of England there never passed four years without a most horrible treason tending to disturb the entire kingdom.

■ Written by Robert Cecil, Earl of Salisbury, in 1606.

What do you think?

3 **a)** Make a note of the following:
- the three things that most concern your character about religion in England
- the three things that most concern your character about how the country is ruled.

b) Compare your worries with those of your partner's character. In what ways are your concerns similar or different? Why do you think they are similar or different?

Now try this

4 Why might the king find it difficult to please everyone about religion?

b) What advice would your character give to King James' son, Charles, about how to rule well?

1.1b

In this lesson you will:

- learn about the disagreements between King Charles I and Parliament

- decide whether King Charles' decisions led to civil war.

Charles I and the road to war

Soon after Charles I became king in 1625, serious arguments broke out between him and Parliament.

a

To him pudel

Bite him peper

Cavalier Dog

Roundhead Curr

- This cartoon called 'Cavalier dog vs Roundhead curr' was created at some point between 1645 and 1648.

? *Look at source a. What can you see in this cartoon? Who do the two groups of people represent? What do you think the cartoon is trying to say about the situation in England at this time?*

Your turn ...

1 King Charles I made many decisions in the run-up to the Civil War in 1642. Work through **problems 1–4**. Which decisions would your character (who you picked in Lesson 1.1a) have wanted the king to make?

Problem 1, 1637: Punishing critics

Many Puritans have criticised Charles for marrying a Catholic and allowing Catholic advisers at court. They even accused him of being a secret Catholic. In 1637 three Puritans were arrested for printing pamphlets criticising changes to the Church of England, as they thought they made it more Catholic. The three men were put on trial and found guilty.

How should you punish critics?

a) Execute them. They have criticised the king in public.

b) Brand them with the initials 'SL' (standing for 'seditious libeller', meaning 'dangerous liar') and have their ears cut off.

c) Imprison them.

Problem 2, 1637: Raising money

The king is often very short of money. Parliament won't let him raise taxes unless he agrees to give them more power over religion and foreign policy. Kings were only allowed to collect taxes without Parliament's approval in emergencies, such as war. Since 1626 Charles I has collected a tax to pay for the navy, because England was at war with Spain.
This tax was called 'Ship Money'.

After the war, should Charles continue to demand 'Ship Money'?

a) No. He should call a new Parliament and ask them to give permission for taxes to be collected.

b) Yes. He should continue to collect 'Ship Money' without Parliament's consent from people throughout England, not just those living in coastal towns. It is up to the king to decide when it is an emergency.

c) Yes. He should continue to collect 'Ship Money' without Parliament's consent but reduce the amount and demand only that people who live in coastal towns pay.

Problem 3, 1640:
Scottish churches and the Earl of Strafford

Charles has forced changes on the Scottish Church which has led to war with Scotland. He needs money to pay for this war and so calls a new Parliament. However, Parliament refuses to give Charles the money unless he promises to hand over his favourite adviser, the Earl of Strafford, for punishment.

What should Charles do?

a) Reject all of Parliament's demands. Charles is king by divine right.

b) Hand over Strafford to Parliament, promise to take advice from Parliament at least every three years and agree that taxes raised without Parliament's consent are illegal.

c) Refuse to hand over Stafford and raise taxes without the consent of Parliament.

Problem 4, 1642:
Dealing with opposition in Parliament

In October 1641 a rebellion breaks out in Ireland. Charles now needs more money to fight the Irish. However, some MPs are refusing to pay for an army that the king is going to lead. They are afraid he will use the army against his opponents in Parliament and suggest that Parliament should be in charge instead.

What should the king do with the MPs who oppose him?

a) Agree to Parliament's demands in return for an army to send to Ireland.

b) Arrest the five ringleaders on their way to the House of Commons.

c) Arrest the five ringleaders by entering the House of Commons with armed soldiers, even though bringing weapons into Parliament is illegal.

Were you right?

2 Did your decisions match those made by Charles I (see the bottom of the page)?

3 How might your character have felt about Charles' decisions?

Over to you ...

4 Imagine you are King Charles. Write a brief letter to Parliament, defending your decisions.

Charles vs Parliament

It was perhaps no surprise that after Charles' attempt to arrest the five MPs, parliament refused to trust him to be in command of the army to use against the Irish Rebellion. Parliament put itself in control of the army. Charles could not tolerate such a huge limitation of his power and raised his own army. At this point, even some MPs felt that parliament had gone too far and joined the king's side.

After both sides had an army, it was only a matter of time before civil war broke out. It began in August 1642 when King Charles declared war on Parliament.

Now try this

5 Design a propaganda leaflet for Parliament at the start of the Civil War. The aim of the leaflet is to get support by outlining the bad decisions and actions made by the others in the lead-up to the war. Remember to organise your information into sections and to give examples to support your arguments.

Here are the decisions that Charles took:	Problem 1 = b	Problem 2 = b	Problem 3 = b	Problem 4 = c

In this lesson you will:

In this lesson you will:

- find out about the different sides in the Civil War: the Parliamentarians and the Royalists

- use sources to discover how Parliament used propaganda to help win the war.

King or Parliament?

Civil war broke out in 1642 and across the country people had to make the difficult decision whether to support King Charles I or Parliament.

? *What conclusions can you draw from this map?*

Both sides imposed conscription and taxes in the areas they controlled to fund their armies.

■ *This map shows the main areas of support for both the king and parliament.*

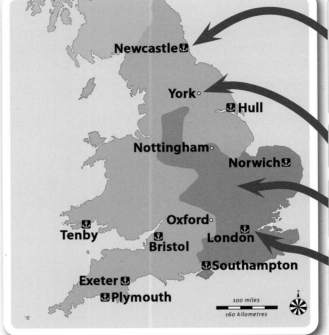

- The Earl of Newcastle, like many wealthy lords, supported Charles; he raised and equipped a small army to fight for the king.

- The population of York was 10,000

- The south-east was the wealthiest region.

- London was wealthiest city with a population of 400,000.

Support for King

⚓ Major ports held by Parliament

Support for Parliament

Key words

Parliamentarian
Supporter of Parliament in the Civil War. They were also known as 'roundheads' because of their short haircuts.

Royalist
Supporters of King Charles. They were also known as Cavaliers.

Issue	For king	For Parliament
Religion	Protestant/ Anglican/ Catholic	Protestant/Strict Protestant/ Puritan
Geography	North and west of England Oxford York Wales Ireland Highlands of Scotland	South and east of England London Coastal towns Central and southern Scotland
Wealth/job (most people would fight on the same side as their boss or landlord)	Wealthy landowners Some merchants	Some landowners Most merchants
Personal political opinion	Believed in the divine right of kings	Believed Parliament should have more power

1 Remind yourself of the character which you chose in Lesson 1.1a and used again in Lesson 1.1b. Now look at the table opposite. Which side would your character support? Why?

2 Now decide who the following people would have supported?

- **James Lawley**, a wealthy Protestant landowner, living near Dundee.
- **Robert Jackson**, a skilled London cloth maker. He is a Puritan.
- **Matthew Lyth**, a farmer in south England. He believes in the divine right, and his landlord supports Parliament.

Once people had chosen sides, each side wanted to gain as much support as it could and to show how bad the actions of the other side were. Propaganda pamphlets produced by Parliament told stories of terrible actions taken by **Royalist** troops. But could these stories be trusted?

■ **Parliamentarian** *propaganda published in 1644 showing Royalist soldiers killing children.*

■ *An image of Prince Rupert, commander of the Royalist cavalry. This picture is taken from a pamphlet entitled 'The Cruel Practices of Prince Rupert', published in 1643.*

■ *An image of Royalist soldiers looting a church, published during the Civil War.*

Use your eyes!

3 Look at **sources a–c**, which all show Royalist soldiers.

a) What are the soldiers doing and what impression do you get of these troops?

b) How do you think these pictures might have affected people who were still deciding which side to support?

How the war was reported

The English Civil War saw both large set-piece battles and many smaller skirmishes and sieges that took place across the country. These events were reported by both sides but each side often gave very different impressions!

Successful storming of Cirencester

Our men took many prisoners, among whom were two ministers [churchmen] armed with sword and pistols. Thus was Cirencester taken with the loss of less than 20 men on our side. The numbers of the enemy killed was about 300, although others think more. The prisoners we brought away numbered about 1,200, which shows the mercy of the Royalists, as the captives themselves acknowledge. Among the prisoners were some 160 wounded whom the prince next day sent his surgeon and doctor to dress and visit.

■ *Extract from a Royalist pamphlet about the storming of Cirencester in February 1643.*

Cruel capture of Cirencester

At about 12 o'clock a furious assault began. Of the town forces there were not above 20 killed. The number of prisoners that they took was between eleven and 1,200, among whom were two godly ministers. They stripped many of the prisoners and though many of them were wounded and weary, their friends were not allowed to bring them a cup of water. They shamefully abused the two ministers taunting them: 'Where is your god now?' The value of the pillage of the town is very great, to the utter ruin of many hundred families.

■ *Extract from a Parliamentarian pamphlet about the storming of Cirencester in February 1643.*

Compare the sources

4 Read **sources d** and **e** about the attack on Cirencester.

   a) Do they agree or disagree about what happened? Use a table like the one below to record what you find out.

Similarities between sources	Differences between sources

   b) How can you explain the differences between the sources? Think carefully about the origin of each one (who wrote it), and the purpose (why it was written). What does this tell you about the sources?

   c) Why might **sources d** and **e** present different interpretations of what happened at Cirencester? Remember to look at the origin of the sources. How might each side have used these sources to convince people to support them?

Factfile

Name: Brilliana Harley

Who she was:
Brilliana Harley and her husband, Robert, were wealthy people. They lived at Brampton Castle in Herefordshire – a county in which many people supported the Royalists.

■ Brilliana Harley.

About her husband:
Brilliana's husband was an MP and was very friendly with those men in Parliament who criticised King Charles I.

? **Which side do you think Brilliana Harley would have supported? Why**

The Harleys actually supported Parliament. While Robert was away from home in the war, Brilliana was left to defend the castle. In 1642 Royalist troops launched a siege of Brampton Castle in which Brilliana was sheltering with some servants and her three teenage children. During the siege she wrote letters to her eldest son, Ned (see **sources f–h**).

f
13 December 1642
My heart has been in no rest since you went. I confess I was never so full of sorrow. I fear the provision of corn and malt will not hold out, if this siege continues; and they say they will burn my barns; and my fear is that they will place soldiers so near me that there will be no going out.

■ Extracts from Brilliana Harley's letters to her son, Ned, which she wrote during 1642 and 1643.

g
14 February 1643
Now the Royalists say they will starve me out of my house. They say they will drive away the cattle, and then I shall have nothing to live on. Their aim is to enforce me to let those men I have go that they might then seize on my house and cut our throats.

h
6 May 1643
My servant, honest Peter, is taken by the Royalists. My friend told me that she heard that six soldiers set upon him, and he was wounded in the head and shoulder and is in prison in Ludlow. Rumour says he is badly treated. A Lieutenant called Marrow comes everyday and kicks him up and down, and they lay him in a dungeon on foul straw.

Over to you ...

5 Read **sources f–h**, then answer these questions.

a) Why might Parliament have wanted to use Brilliana's letters as part of their propaganda?

b) Can we be certain of everything bad that Brilliana writes about the Royalists in **source h**? Think about where she got her information from.

c) Brilliana's letters were written to her son, Ned. Do you think this makes them more or less truthful about what the Royalists were really like?

d) How reliable do you think Brilliana's letters are in telling us about the Royalists?
i) Totally reliable. **ii)** Quite reliable but exaggerated.
iii) Not at all reliable. Explain your answer by referring to the origin and purpose of the letters.

In conclusion ...

6 Write a letter from a Parliamentarian explaining why propaganda was so important to Parliament winning the Civil War. Refer to how it helped to them gain supporters and how it was used to weaken the Royalists.

7 You are a modern historian giving advice to a student who wants to find out about the Royalists in the Civil War. How and why would you advise them to be careful when using some of the primary sources in this lesson? You should refer to the nature, origin and purpose of the sources.

1.1d

In this lesson you will:

In this lesson you will:

- find out what happened at the Battle of Naseby

- identify the most important reasons why Parliament won the Battle of Naseby and the Civil War.

Eyewitness: Naseby

Your character (see Lessons 1.1a–c) has made it to June 1645 and the Battle of Naseby! This was an important turning point in the Civil War because it was a major victory for Parliament's army.

Look and think

1 Read through the information on the battle map to find out what happened during this battle.

   a) In pairs, decide which factors and decisions you think helped Parliament to win the battle.

   b) What mistakes do you think the Royalists made?

? *How would your character react to news of a victory for Parliament?*

Prince Rupert: a brave and charismatic leader, but sometimes rash and foolhardy.

Royalist starting position: at the bottom of a hill, protected by a ridge but this limited their view of the enemy.

King Charles The king tried to lead some survivors in a cavalry charge but was stopped by his own advisers.

After the battle: Parliament captured letters showing how the king planned to get help from the Irish by giving Catholics greater rights in Ireland. Parliament published these letters, which caused the king to lose further support from Protestants in England.

Cavalry

Parliament: 6,000
Royalists: 4,100

Although outnumbered, Prince Rupert still attacked Parliament. It was only after the attack that the Royalists saw just how outnumbered they were but it was too late to turn back.

Parliamentarian cavalry: Unlike the Royalist cavalry, they were well disciplined and reformed after each successful charge.

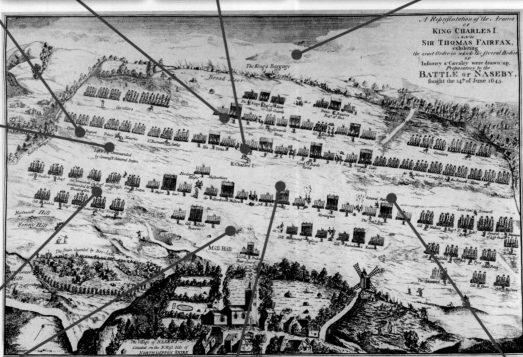

Parliamentarian starting position: at the top of a hill. A ridge obscured their view of the enemy.

Infantry

Royalists: 3,300 men but they were not well funded, and many were **conscripts**.

Parliament: 7,000 men who were paid a good salary. They were well trained, disciplined and had good morale.

The infantry marched to attack each other. Then Parliamentarian cavalry attacked from both sides and the Royalist infantry was defeated.

Parliamentary leaders: Fairfax, Cromwell and Ireton were all experienced and skilful commanders.

Prioritise

2 Sort your ideas from task 1 into a table like the one below. For all categories give each army a score out of 5 (5 = excellent; 0 = hopeless) to show, in your opinion, the most important reason to explain why Parliament won the Civil War. Make sure you give a reason for each score.

Category	Royalists	Parliamentarians
Quality of leadership		
Size, training and discipline of troops		
Raising men, money and supplies		
Making useful alliances		

Key words

Conscripts
People who are forced to serve in the armed forces.

After the battle

After the Battle of Naseby, the Parliamentarians were able to take control of much of western England, which gave them more land, people and resources. This was important because it meant their army was more confident, larger and better supplied than the Royalist army.

Parliament finally won the war in 1648 when they took Charles prisoner for a second time. Parliament decided to put the king on trial for treason against the nation.

Argue a case

3 Discuss with another pair which of the four categories in your table was most important in explaining why Parliament won the Civil War. If you disagree with their choice, you need to use evidence to back up your choice.

4 Finally, take a class vote on what the most important reason was.

Back to the start

Design a pamphlet or poster produced by Parliament to encourage men to join its army. Organise it into key sections and look back over the work you have done throughout Lessons 1.1a–d to find information. You could include sections such as:

● how the Royalist troops caused damage and destruction

● why Parliament will win (use information you have learned in this lesson).

You might also want to ask: 'Why fight for Parliament?' (Look through this enquiry for the reasons Parliament went to war with Charles in the first place).

1.1e

Taking it further!

How do you punish a king?

It is January 1649 and after years of Civil War, Parliament is victorious and King Charles I is a prisoner. The question now is what to do with him? Read through the speech bubbles, which explain what happened after the war.

> Parliament has been trying for years to make a deal with Charles I to share power more fairly. He always refuses.

> The Civil War was Charles' fault. He made a deal with the Scots to invade England in 1648.

> Charles declared war on Parliament in 1642.

> Charles tried to get help from Holland and other foreign rulers during the Civil War.

> Other monarchs in Europe might invade England to help Charles.

> Charles ruled badly, taxing the people heavily and refusing to take advice from Parliament.

> Charles escaped from prison in 1647. He might try again.

> There are still many Royalists in England who might stir up rebellion and try to put the king back on the throne.

> According to the law, the king is the most powerful judge in England, so it is illegal for Parliament to put a king on trial and judge him.

> Parliament has become power-hungry. Who's to say it will do any better than the king?

> Parliament pushed Charles into declaring war in the first place by making unreasonable demands.

> God will punish those who kill a king who is ruler by divine right.

> Charles' eldest son, also called Charles, is 19 years old and living in France. Although he fought for his father in the early years of the Civil War, we know little about his personality or political beliefs.

> Charles believes that he is king by divine right, and that it would be wrong for him to give any of his God-given power to Parliament.

What should happen to Charles?

1 Imagine you have been asked to represent one group of MPs. You can select from the following:

- **Radical/Puritan MPs:** they want to execute the king.
- **Moderate MPs:** they want to remove Charles but keep a monarchy.
- **Royalist Sympathiser MPs:** they want to reinstate the king.

Which evidence would you select to make your case for what should happen to Charles?

2 Once you have selected your evidence, think about what your opponents might say. How will you respond to their arguments?

Did you know?

The judge at Charles' trial had his hat reinforced with steel because he was so frightened that he might be attacked by a Royalist.

Charles I's trial

Parliament decided that Charles was untrustworthy and a danger to the peace of England. He was put on trial in January 1649 accused of High Treason against the nation.

Charles argued that the trial was illegal and that he could not be tried by Parliament. However, the decision was taken that he was guilty of High Treason against the nation, the sentence for which was death. Charles I was beheaded on 30 January 1649.

? *Think back to the character that you selected at the start of this enquiry. Would your character agree or disagree with the outcome of the trial? Why? Why not?*

Design a pamphlet

3 Design a pamphlet produced by Parliament setting out the reasons why the execution of the king was the only option. You should organise your points into key sections, such as:

- why Charles was guilty of the charges against him
- why his own actions meant less extreme action would be risky.

Give examples to support your points.

In this lesson you will:

- find out what life was like during the rule of Oliver Cromwell and King Charles II

- make a judgement about which ruler your character would have preferred.

Key words

Lord Protector

The title given to Oliver Cromwell in 1653 which gave him the power to rule England.

1.2a Parliament or king?

- *Oliver Cromwell, **Lord Protector** of England, 1653–1658. Cromwell instructed the artist to 'paint my picture truly like me and not flatter me at all. Show all the roughness, pimples, warts and all.'*

- *This painting shows King Charles II (1660–1685) at his court. Charles was nicknamed the 'Merrie Monarch' because he enjoyed leisure time and women. (He had more than seven mistresses!)*

? **Look at sources a and b. What are the differences in how these rulers are shown? With a partner, make a list of three differences.**

Sources c–h tell us more about what Oliver Cromwell and Charles II were like and how they ruled England.

c Cromwell restored justice according to the law, and his own court was well ordered so no drunkard, nor anyone guilty of bribery, was to be found there without severe punishment. Trade began again to prosper; and in a word, gentle peace to flourish all over England.

- *Written by George Bate, Cromwell's physician (doctor), after the death of Cromwell.*

d We declare that we shall from time to time allow a sufficient number of places in all parts of the kingdom, for the use of those who do not conform to the Church of England, to meet and assemble in.

- *Adapted from the Declaration of Indulgence, 1672. This section describes the law passed by Charles II to end the persecution of people who did not want to attend Church of England services.*

e Cromwell and his army grew greedy with their power, and invented a thousand tricks of government. Not finding one parliament in agreement with him, he shut them down.

- *Written by Lucy Hutchinson in her book* The Life of Colonel Hutchinson *in 1670 and published in 1806. Cromwell shut Parliament down on a number of occasions when he disagreed with it and used his soldiers to impose order in the countryside.*

f

The king mixed himself among the crowd, allowed every man to speak to him as he pleased, went hawking in the mornings, to cock fights or foot races in the afternoons (if there were no horse races), and to plays in the evenings.

■ *Description by Sir John Reresby (1634–89) of how Charles II spent his final years written during his lifetime and published in 1734.*

g

■ *A playing card from 1678 showing the execution of five Catholics accused of plotting to assassinate Charles II. There was widespread fear of a Catholic Plot in 1678 and in total fifteen, probably innocent, Catholics were executed. Many suspected Catholics were driven out of London.*

h

■ *A pamphlet from 1653 showing different reactions to the banning of Christmas celebrations since 1647. These celebrations were banned because it was felt they distracted from prayer.*

Rate the rulers

1 Use **sources c–h** to help you, to rates both Charles and Cromwell.

As the character you chose for yourself in Lesson 1.1a, award marks out of 10 for Cromwell's reign. Then do the same for Charles II. Make sure you can justify the rating you have given to each ruler. You should rate them out of 10 (10 being the best mark) on these categories:

Religious freedom; Fun; Entertainment and leisure; Having your say (representation and Parliament); Law and Order; Personality.

Decision time

2 Which ruler would your character have preferred to live under? Remember that some issues might be of more importance to your character than others. Give reasons for your character's preferred ruler.

Back in character!

3 Write a diary entry of about 250 words for your character remembering Charles II's return to England. As you write, think about these questions.

● Would your character be pleased that the monarchy had come back? Why? Would they regret any aspect of the end of Cromwell's rule?

1.2b

In this lesson you will:

- find out what happened in 1688 when William of Orange claimed the throne

- investigate whether William's claim to the throne was popular in England.

1.2b England invaded!

■ *William of Orange's army lands at Brixham in Devon.*

Newsflash! The forces of William, Prince of Orange, the son-in-law of King James II, have been spotted off the south coast. They are believed to be heading towards Torbay in Devon. It is rumoured that William is here to claim the English crown.

? *You are a news reporter who has been sent to the south coast to cover this breaking story. What will be your first question? Why?*

Ask some questions

1 Read through the statements below.

  a) As a reporter, make a list of of other questions to ask, then share it with your partner. Add any extra questions to your list, so you can get as much information as possible. Will you ask everyone the same thing?

  b) Use the statements to answer your questions so that you can put together your report. Decide whether your story is for or against the invasion.

2 Create a story board for your news report. Divide it into these key sections:

- Why did William come?
- Was it an invasion or was he invited?
- Who was with him?
- Will William as king be good news for England?

Remember, what you include will depend on whether you are *for* or *against* William!

Lord John Churchill, Duke of Marlborough – a commander in James II's army.
I have slipped away from King James' camp and am on my way to offer my loyalty to William of Orange. I have been worried for some time that James II, who is a Catholic, is trying to make England a Catholic country. As a Protestant, I must support William, who has promised to defend Protestantism if he becomes king. James is unpopular so I am sure William will win, and he may reward me for my support.

John Drummond, Earl of Melford – a Scottish nobleman who had been given a large amount of land in Scotland by James II
I am outraged by news that William of Orange has landed in England and is claiming the throne! James II is the rightful king because he is the brother of the previous king, Charles II. William is invading and should be punished as a traitor. I will stand by James, even if this means going into exile, until we can prepare forces to return and take back the throne!

Henry Compton, the former Bishop of London
I am delighted that William of Orange has taken up our invitation to become king. Those who say William is launching an invasion are quite wrong. He was invited by myself and other MPs to save the country from James II's bad rule. William has a claim to the throne too, because he is married to James II's daughter. I was dismissed from my position of Bishop of London by James for criticising James' pro-Catholic policies. I hope that William, who has promised to support Protestantism and to listen to the advice of Parliament, will give me back my job.

Anne Hamilton, a Catholic noble woman
William of Orange has no right to try to become King of England. He is only married to James II's daughter, Mary, and has no direct claim himself. It is all a plot by Protestants in Parliament to get rid of James because he is a Catholic. Life for Catholics in England has improved under James II's rule. I am worried that the persecution of Catholics will begin again if William becomes king.

b **William promised to:**

- maintain the Protestant religion
- call a free Parliament, which would be not be banned from discussing any political issues, and from which he would take advice before raising taxes and passing laws
- investigate the legitimacy of James II's recently born son.

■ *Summary of the Declaration of the Hague written by William of Orange to explain why he claimed the throne. More than 60,000 copies were printed and distributed in England in 1688.*

Write a clear account

3   Write a dialogue for an interview with one of the witnesses.

Remember, before interviewing the witness, you will need to set the scene. You might also want to question whether the opinions of the witnesses are based on what they think will be better for England or, more selfishly, what will be better for themselves!

Tell the story

4   Write a newspaper report to tell people what has happened. Don't forget to include an eye-catching headline so that people will want to read your story!

Next Lesson

In this lesson you will:

- find out the reasons for and against a union between Scotland and England in 1707

- judge whether the union with England was to the advantage of Scotland.

1.3a Were Scottish MPs bribed?

? *Read through the statements below. Which support the argument in favour of a union between England and Scotland? Which support the argument against it?*

> Scotland will lose independence. England will be making decisions on Scotland's behalf.

> Scotland and France have often been allies in the past. It could be disastrous for England if this happened again.

> Protestant Scottish Lowlanders dislike the Scottish Catholic Highlanders more than they dislike the English. They feel threatened by the Highlanders.

> Scottish merchants will be able to trade on equal terms with countries in England's empire.

> The Anglican Church in England might not accept the Scottish Presbyterian Church.

> Many English merchants do not want to share their trading rights with the Scots.

> England wants to have only Protestant kings and queens. There is the possibility that the Scots might choose a Catholic king.

> England has a large army so Scotland will be more secure.

Act of Union

England and Scotland were ruled by the same king for the first time in 1603 when James VI of Scotland also became King of England. However, they remained two separate countries until 1707 when Members of the Scottish Parliament agreed to the Act of Union.

Some accused the Scottish MPs who agreed to the union of being traitors to Scotland and claimed they were bribed. You need to investigate these claims and by the end of this lesson decide whether you think the MPs were bribed (and find evidence for this) or whether there were good reasons at the time for the Act of Union.

Evidence A: from George Lockhart of Carnwath, a Scottish MP in 1707 who strongly opposed the union with England.
Queen Anne has given more than £20,000 to Members of the Scottish Parliament who will support a union with England. The Duke of Queensberry received £12,325 for his support, and William Seton, who was against union in 1703, changed his mind after he was given £100 a year in 1704. Can this be a coincidence?

Evidence B: from William Seton of Pitmedden, a Scottish MP in 1707 who supported the union with England.
Scotland is behind all the other nations of Europe in wealth. This nation is poor because it does not have enough military force to protect its trade. Scotland's small army and navy means it is vulnerable to attack. In 1695 and 1706 Scotland had to rely on help from the English against attacks on trading ships by French pirates.

Evidence C: a question of bribery.
The Duke of Queensbury did receive large amounts of money from the English, but he was already firmly in favour of the union. Many of the other men received payments of £50 or less, and this may not have been decisive in changing their point of view. Some of them were entitled to receive money from England as part of their jobs anyway.

Evidence D: the importance of English trade to Scotland.
A law called the Aliens Act, which would have come into effect if the Scots had not agreed to a union with England, was designed to ban the import of goods from Scotland into England. This would have damaged Scottish trade because they relied on importing goods into England. For example, more than half of Scotland's main exports of linen cloth and cattle were sold in England.

Evidence E: extracts of the terms of the Act of Union of 1707.
- Free trade between Scotland and England.
- The same taxes would be paid in England and Scotland, with the following exceptions:
  - the Scottish would pay a lower tax on salt than the English
  - the Scottish would not have to pay window tax until 1 August 1710
  - the Scottish would not have to pay coal tax until 30 September 1710 (this was in recognition of the fact that Scotland was not as rich as England).
- Scotland would no longer have its own Parliament, but would send 45 representatives to the Parliament in London.

Your turn ...

1 In pairs write down five questions you would want to ask if you were to interview one of the MPs accused of bribery. Now share your list with another pair and add more ideas.

Explain your reasons

2 Write a complaint to one of the Scottish MPs who is in favour of the Union with England setting down why you think the Union would be a bad thing.

Defend yourself!

3 Imagine you are one of the Scottish MPs who has to defend themselves against charges of bribery. How will you respond to the charges? Use examples from the evidence to support your point of view.

Think about how you can show that you did not receive money illegally and give reasons why you might think the union with England was a good idea.

In this lesson you will:

- find out what happened when Bonnie Prince Charlie arrived in Scotland

- decide whether you think he was brave or foolish.

Was Bonnie Prince Charlie brave or foolish?

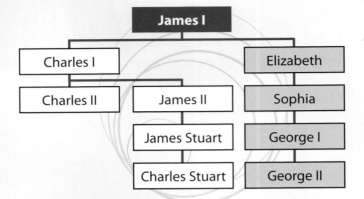

```
                    James I
        ┌──────────────┴──────────────┐
    Charles I                      Elizabeth
        │                             │
    Charles II      James II        Sophia
                       │              │
                  James Stuart      George I
                       │              │
                  Charles Stuart    George II
```

? Who do you think had a better claim to the throne: Charles Stuart or George II? Why?

Key words

Jacobites
The name given to those who belived that James II and his descendants were the rightful Kings of England and Scotland.

Bonnie Prince Charlie

After the Act of Union in 1707, some Scots disliked being ruled by the English king and caused trouble by taking part in revolts. The most serious took place in 1745, when Bonnie Prince Charlie led a rebellion in Scotland to claim the throne from George II. Bonnie Prince Charlie believed he was the rightful King of Britain. He was descended from King James II who had been removed from the throne in 1688 because he was a Catholic.

Look carefully

1 Look at **source a**. What impression does it give you of what Bonnie Prince Charlie might have been like? Make a list of words or phrases that you would use to describe him.

a

■ *An image of Bonnie Prince Charlie, painted in 1749.*

Compare information

2 Read the information about Bonnie Prince Charlie on the map opposite.

Statement 1: Bonnie Prince Charlie was not particularly popular, was a bad military leader and a coward who needlessly risked the lives of his supporters in his attempt to claim the throne.

Statement 2: Bonnie Prince Charlie was popular, brave and right to attempt to gain the throne.

a) Which statement do you most agree with? Why? Select information from this lesson to back up your opinion.

b) Discuss your choice with a partner. If they disagree with you, try to convince them that you are right!

1 Bonnie Prince Charlie first landed in Scotland with just one ship and 700 supporters.

2 Only a few Catholic Highland clans came to meet Charlie, and he lacked support from the mainly Protestant people of the Scottish lowlands.

3 Charlie was joined by more Highland clans as he marched through Scotland. Eventually he had more than 6,000 supporters.

4 The Government had only a small army based in Scotland at the time. Charlie easily beat them at the Battle of Prestonpans.

8 After the defeat Charlie did not try to regroup his men and lead them to safety. Instead, he fled to the Isle of Skye disguised as a woman. He then fled to Italy and did not return to Scotland.

7 Charlie waited for the Government troops at Culloden. The usually fearsome charge of the Highlanders failed because of the rain-soaked boggy ground. The Government took just over 1 hour to beat the Jacobites.

6 Charlie was advised to retreat into the Scottish Highlands to hide from the Government troops that were following them. Charlie ignored their advice and decided to fight.

5 Charlie marched to Derby. But, the Government troops in London outnumbered the Jacobites. The Highland clan chiefs decided to retreat to Scotland. Charlie couldn't stop them but he flew into a rage when he heard their decision.

Inverness Culloden
Edinburgh Prestonpans
Derby
London

100 miles
160 kilometres

In conclusion ...

3 Write an obituary for Bonnie Prince Charlie following his death in 1788 in Rome. Make sure you:

a) describe the popular image of him as a Scottish hero and as the man who should have been king

b) explain whether you agree with these views

c) use examples from his life to support your points.

Back to the start

In 1999 Scotland was given its own Parliament again for the first time since 1707. The Scottish Parliament has the power to make laws for Scotland on issues including: education, healthcare, prisons, transport, agriculture and fishing, the police and tourism. Issues such as taxation and foreign policy that affect the whole of the United Kingdom are still decided in the British Parliament in London.

What are the benefits (if any) of Scotland having a separate parliament again?

Next lesson

In this lesson you will:

- investigate Lord Macartney's visit to China and the first formal meeting of the British and Chinese empires
- use sources to compare and contrast the Chinese and British ideas about empire.

China: the 'Middle Kingdom'

? *Let us now look elsewhere in the world. What do you know about China today?*

The Chinese word for China is 'shogun'. This literally means 'central' or 'middle kingdom'. For centuries China had assumed it was at the centre of the world and all other countries were inferior.

Then during the Qing Dynasty period (from 1644 onwards) the Chinese and British empires met formally for the first time. After 1759 Europeans were only allowed to trade in one city and could only stay long enough to conduct their business. In 1793, Lord Macartney, Ambassador of George III of England, visited China to try to convince Emperor Qianlong to allow British ambassadors and merchants to settle in China and control British business from there.

a

■ *Macartney's arrival procession to meet the Chinese Emperor, Qianlong, in 1793.*

Lord Macartney took 10 months to reach Beijing where he attended many banquets. From Beijing, Macartney travelled by road in his own British carriage to the palace where the emperor was staying. He was accompanied all the way by two very high-ranking **mandarins**.

On the way, Macartney and his party stopped to look at the Great Wall of China and were amazed. The mandarins quickly and nervously put him back on the right road. As they neared the palace the party formed a huge procession – mandarins followed by British soldiers, followed by servants and musicians, followed by Macartney and his secretary Sir George Staunton.

Key words

Envoy
A special representative who visits a foreign country.

Mandarin
Officials in the Chinese civil service.

Write home

1 Macartney's secretary, Sir George Staunton, took his son with him. Imagine you are Staunton's son. Write a postcard back home to your family. Using **sources a** and **b** and the information above, describe the sights, atmosphere and events of the journey and arrival in as much detail as possible.

Qing rulers

Qing rulers demanded that ambassadors from foreign countries take part in the 'tributary system'. This meant showing subservience to Chinese rulers included kowtowing – (kneeling) three times, then lying fully face down on the floor and touching the ground with your forehead three times. The emperor would then receive gifts. In return, Qing rulers would give benefits to these countries such as allowing them to trade in China.

■ *Lord Macartney meeting Emperor Qianlong, painted in 1793.*

Use the source

2 Look carefully at **source b**, then answer the following questions.

  a) How does Lord Macartney greet Emperor Qianlong?

  b) How do you think he would have greeted his own king, George III?

  c) Lord Macartney said he would only perform the kowtow if a Chinese person of his rank kowtowed to a picture of King George. The Chinese refused. If he had performed the kowtow, what would this have said about the power of the Chinese emperor compared to the power of King George?

c
The kings of the many nations come by land and sea with all sorts of precious things. Consequently there is nothing we lack, as your principle **envoy** and others have themselves observed. We have never set much store on strange objects, nor do we need any more of your country's manufactured goods.

■ *Extract from a letter from Emperor Qianlong to King George III of England on the return of Lord Macartney, 1793.*

d
England is not the only barbarian land that wishes to establish trade with our empire. Supposing that other nations were all to imitate your evil example and ask me to present them each and all with a site for trading purposes, how could I possibly agree?

■ *Extract from a letter from Emperor Qianlong to King George III of England on the return of Lord Macartney, 1793.*

A failed mission

Britain wanted links with the Chinese court and wanted English merchants to be able to trade in other parts of China. Although the Chinese were good hosts, the mission failed.

In conclusion ...

3 Read **source c**. What reasons did Emperor Qianlong give for the failure of the mission?

4 **a)** Look again at **sources a–d**. What do they tell you about the following?

  ● The Chinese view of empire?

  ● The British view of empire?

  b) How are the two countries' views similar and different?

1.4b

In this lesson you will:

In this lesson you will:

- investigate the government and bureaucracy of Qing Dynasty China

- analyse the significance of the Qing system of governance for those who lived under it.

How was China ruled?

How is a School run?

Here are four groups from your school.

- Teachers
- Students
- Heads and Deputies
- Governors

From 1662 to1795 the Qing Dynasty was ruled by only three emperors. All three worked hard and ran the country well.

 How is your school run? Use the four groups listed here to show who reports to who and who's responsible for who by drawing a chart. Use one colour arrow for reporting and another colour arrow for responsibility.

How was the Qing Dynasty run?

The emperor was the absolute ruler. All government workers were divided into six Boards and the Central Government Command was in charge of overseeing the following Boards on behalf of the emperor.

- Board of Civil Appointments: promoted and fired staff in the government.

- Board of Finance: taxes, land ownership and government money.

- Board of Rites: correct court behaviour the Civil Examination that had to be taken by all government officials.

- Board of War: some of the fighting forces. The emperor himself controlled the rest.

- Board of Punishments: law and order.

- Board of Works: government building projects and minting of all coins.

Each Board was headed by two Supreme Secretaries and aided by four Assistant Secretaries. The Qing Dynasty also introduced a Feudatory Affairs Office to oversee the welfare of all the groups that came under Qing control as the Chinese Empire expanded.

Read and think

1 Create a flow chart or diagram to illustrate how the Qing Empire was governed.

The Board of Punishment

One of the main functions of the Qing Government, like any other government, was to maintain order and punish crime. From time to time, the emperor would spare someone punishment to show he was not too harsh.

(a)

Five punishments

1 Beating with a light bamboo stick.

2 Beating with a heavy bamboo stick.

3 Penal servitude (slavery).

4 Exile.

5 Penalty of death.

■ *Taken from Article 1 of the Qing Legal Code.*

The ten great wrongs

1 Plotting rebellion.
2 Plotting to overthrowing the emperor.
3 Plotting treason.
4 Killing close family.
5 Dismembering a person or making poisons.
6 Lack of respect (making mistakes while preparing food).
7 Cursing one's parents or grand parents.
8 Killing relatives.
9 Killing your teacher or a superior officer.
10 Sexual relations with your own family.

■ *Article 2 of the Qing Legal Code.*

■ *A criminal being punished in China in 1804.*

Discussion time

2 Look carefully at **sources a–c**.

a) What do you think are the good points about this system of justice?

b) What do you think are the bad points about this system of justice?

The emperor's judgement failed in his later years. Not only did he pass much of his authority to a young bodyguard he favoured, he also failed to recognise social problems caused by overpopulation. The population had grown from 100 million in 1644 to 430 million in 1850. However, the number of government officials was not increased. Government officials gave responsibilities to less experienced members of staff or gave control of works to local rich gentry.

■ *Written by a modern historian, 2008.*

e By the end of the eighteenth century, Europeans in China worried about a lack of concern for the rights of the accused. In 1773 the Portuguese authorities in Macao arrested an Englishman accused of killing a Chinese man but after finding him innocent, they released him. The Chinese officials insisted that since the victim was Chinese they should have jurisdiction. They arrested him again, found him guilty, and executed him.

■ *Adapted from a modern historian, 1996.*

In conclusion …

3 The whole system of government seemed very ordered throughout the Qing Dynasty. However such a system had a downside.

a) Use **sources d** and **e** to outline what you think the downside may have been of such a system of rule.

b) Both sources are from modern historians. When we look back at events and point out what the issues were, we call this 'hindsight'. Why do you think government officials would not have raised the issues at the time?

Next Lesson

In this lesson you will:

- understand why the British lost control of America in 1781
- identify the short- and long-term causes to explain why the British lost control of America.

? *Which country seems to be triumphant in source a? How can you tell?*

Yorktown and the defeat of the British

a

■ *A painting showing the aftermath of the battle of Yorktown.*

Source a shows the British army in America surrendering to George Washington, the leader of the American troops, after the Battle of Yorktown in 1781. This was the last battle of the American War of Independence. As a result of wining the war the Americans won freedom from British control (most of North America had been ruled as a British colony since the sixteenth century).

The speech bubbles below explain why many Americans were unhappy about being ruled by Britain, and why they were confident of success.

I joined the army because I am angry about the high taxes that the British make us pay. We have no say about taxation because Americans are not allowed to send representatives to the British Parliament. When some Americans in Boston protested against the increased taxes in March 1770, British troops opened fire. Three Americans were killed. It was after I heard about this that I decided to join up.

But it's not just the taxes. The British have also passed acts to close our main harbour at Boston to trade, to prevent our courts from bringing British officials to trial and to force Americans to let British soldiers stay in their homes to keep control.

We also have France as an ally. Since 1778 the French have sent us more than US$1 million of supplies, weapons and troops.

I think we can beat the British. They have to wait for supplies to be sent from England and do not have much support from people in America. But our American troops are tough, passionate and experienced, having fought against the American Indians.

I joined the American army because I was angry at the British telling us what to do. In 1763 they passed a law preventing us from travelling and settling in the lands occupied by the American Indians to the west of the Appalachian Mountains. My ancestors settled in this country, and the British government have no right to tell us where we can and cannot travel and settle.

We are confident in our commander George Washington's leadership, especially since we heard of the success of his surprise attack on the British across the Delaware River on Christmas Day in 1776. He captured 1,000 British prisoners at a cost of only four Americans wounded.

Read and think

1 Read all the speech bubbles for both soldiers.

a) Make a list of the top five reasons why many Americans volunteered to fight against the British. Compare your list with a partner. Do you agree on your five choices? How are your lists different?

b) Use different colours to highlight on your list the causes that are short term and those that are long term.

Over to you ...

2 Design a poster or write a speech encouraging American men to join the American army against the British. Remember to include the reasons why:

● British rule is bad for America

● the Americans will win.

What happened at Yorktown

● Before the Battle of Yorktown the British had won victories at Savannah, Charleston and Camden nearby, taking more than 1,000 American prisoners.

● American troops near Yorktown were reinforced by 3,000 French troops.

● French ships controlled the waters outside Yorktown after they defeated the British navy. This meant that the French rather than the British could supply their troops on land with food and ammunition.

● British troops led by General Cornwallis set up camp on the Yorktown peninsula in 1781. It was a poor choice of location, as they soon found themselves cut off, without supplies and unable to escape.

● Sensing British weakness, George Washington (the American commander) decided to attack Yorktown. He commanded a force of 17,000 and attacked in September. The British were unable to counter-attack or escape, so had to surrender.

Now try this

3 King George III has asked for a report on why Britain lost the American colonies. Imagine you are General Cornwallis, the commander of British forces in America. You need to explain:

● why you lost the Battle of Yorktown

● why it was unlikely that the British could control America forever.

Remember, your job is on the line so you need to make sure you explain events carefully.

In this lesson you will:

■ find out about how life changed in America after the War of Independence

■ judge how far life improved for people in America.

● Key words

Congress
The elected group of politicians responsible for making laws in the USA.

Land of the free?

America fought the American War of Independence against Britain to gain freedom and fairer government. But did the American Revolution mean that there was greater freedom and equality for ordinary people?

Read **source a**, an extract from the American Bill of Rights, that was passed by the US **Congress** in 1789.

? *Do you think the rights listed in this bill are still important today? What rights are not included that you would have expected to see? Do any surprise you?*

a All citizens of America are guaranteed fundamental rights which include: freedom of religion; freedom of press, speech and assembly; the right to keep and bear firearms; the right to a speedy public trial with legal advice and an impartial jury; and protection against cruel punishment.

■ *From the Bill of Rights, 1789.*

Changing lives

It is 1796, the year America gained independence from Britain and seven years after the Bill of Rights was passed. Imagine you have to interview the following people about how their lives have changed since before 1789, when America was ruled as a colony of Britain.

A black former slave from Massachusetts. *During the war, I, like many others, escaped from the plantation where I was a slave and fled to the north. After the war the northern states abolished slavery, so I was made free. However, the southern states kept their slaves because they relied on them to work on the huge sugar and cotton plantations. Although I am free, I am still not treated equally. I am not allowed to vote, it is hard to find well-paid work and I have no real education because I used to be a slave.*

A New York trader. *The British used to make us pay high taxes on goods, but we don't have to pay these now. Now we can elect American men to Congress to make laws on our behalf. I, like all men who own their own house and land, have the vote. This makes me feel like the government will pass laws which are in my best interest because they will want to keep my support next time I get to vote.*

A poor farm labourer from Virginia. *Not much has changed for us. I work on a farm in Virginia, but because I cannot afford to own the land myself, I am not allowed to vote for the new government. My pay is low, and it is often a struggle to make sure that my wife and four young children are well fed. I have heard that there is land out west, if you can take it from the American Indians. The government is encouraging Americans to go out there and settle the land, so I might take my family out there to begin a new life.*

Land lost by the American Indians

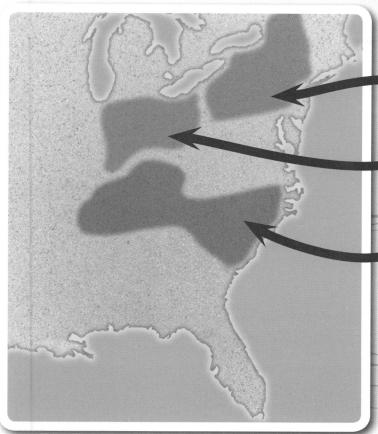

Areas the Iroquois tribe was forced to give up to white settlers in the mid-1780s.

Areas the Cherokee tribe was forced to give up in the mid-1780s.

Areas lost by American Indians following their defeat at the Battle of Fallen Timbers in 1794.

■ *In the 1770s more than 300,000 American settlers set out west into Indian territory to set up new homes.*

Look and read

1 Select information from the characters and sources in this lesson which shows how life in America after the Revolution was:

   a) worse than before for some

   b) still unfair for some

   c) better than before for some.

b

In the new laws I suppose it will be necessary for you to make I desire you would remember the ladies. Do not put such unlimited power into the hands of the husbands. Remember all men would be tyrants [bullies] if they could.

■ *Extract from a letter by Abigail Adams to her husband John Adams, the first vice-president. Women were not given the vote.*

Consider the evidence

2 Look again at all the information in this lesson.

   a) Whose life do you think was changed most by the Revolution? Justify your choice.

   b) Whose life do you think was changed least by the Revolution? Justify your choice.

Argue a case

3 First, design a brochure entitled 'America: Land of the Free' which advertises the benefits of life there after the Revolution. Then, write a letter of complaint in response to your brochure, arguing that America after the Revolution is not the 'Land of the Free'.

1.5c

In this lesson you will:

- discover what happened in France on 14 July 1789

- categorise reasons to explain why the French stormed the Bastille in 1789.

Key words

Absolute/absolutism
A ruler who has unlimited power.

Storming of the Bastille

It was not just in America that people fought for a freer and fairer government. Celebrations are held every year in France on 14 July to remember when the people of Paris attacked and destroyed the royal-owned Bastille prison, on that day in 1789. But why did the people of Paris want to storm the Bastille in 1789 and why was the event so important that it is still remembered today?

a

We hold these to be truths: that all men are created equal; that they have the right to life, liberty and the pursuit of happiness. When a government fails to protect these rights it is the duty of the people to throw off such government.

■ *Extract from* The American Declaration of Independence, *1776.*

? **Read source a. What does it say that might have appealed to people in France and encouraged them to have their own revolution?**

b

■ *The storming of the Bastille prison in Paris in 1789.*

? **The building under attack in source b was used as a prison by the French king. Why might the people want to attack a prison? What shows that the people in the Bastille surrendered? Why do you think the people attacking the Bastille were able to force those inside to surrender?**

Name: King Louis XVI
Born: August 1754, France
Died: January 1793

What he was like:

– Married the Austrian princess, Marie-Antoinette, who was unpopular because she was not French and was extravagant.

– Strongly believed in the divine right of kings and ruled as an **absolute** monarch.

– Didn't want to take advice from anyone. For example, if he wanted to arrest someone all he had to do was to sign and send a sealed letter. That person would not be given the chance to defend themselves at a trial.

– Enjoyed spending time with his children, hunting and collecting clocks. These hobbies often took up more of his time than ruling the country.

– Lived outside Paris in the luxurious Palace of Versailles. He didn't have any idea how ordinary, poor French people lived.

Life in France in the 1780s

Life is very hard for us peasants and harvests recently have been bad. We have to rent our land from a landlord. Rents are high and we have to do unpaid work on the landlord's farm. If I cannot afford to pay the rent, the landlord takes some of my crops as payment. I have to pay to grind my corn in the landlord's mill and bake my bread at his bakery. I also have to pay taxes to the government and the Church but the nobles and clergy often don't pay.

I live in the poorest area of Paris with my wife and four children in a draughty, crowded apartment. I work weaving cloth. We only just make enough money to feed ourselves and this year the price of a loaf of bread has increased again. My brothers were conscripted into the army. They had no choice, unlike the nobles who buy their way out of military service. Recently I had to work, unpaid, fixing the roads in Paris for three days. The nobles do not have to do this labour service.

Make connections

1 Identify the similarities and differences between the complaints made by the peasant and the weaver about the difficulties of life in France in the 1780s.

Make a judgement

2 What complaints do you think the peasant and the weaver might have had about King Louis XVI and his wife Marie-Antoinette? Explain why you think they might have complained about these things.

3 Ordinary people in France clearly had many things to complain about in the 1780s, but many of these problems had existed for years and had not caused a revolution. So why did the people rise up in 1789? Look through the list you made in tasks 1 and 2.

a) Which of these things do you think had been happening for years (the long-term causes)? Underline these in one colour.

b) Which do you think are short-term causes? Underline these in a different colour.

Look at both sides

4 'The French people stormed the Bastille mainly because they were hungry.' Do you agree with this statement? Why?

1.5d

In this lesson you will:

- discover the changes that were made during the French Revolution

- weigh up how much changed for the better in France after the Revolution.

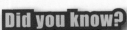
Key words

Fraternity
Friendship and support within a group of people.

Liberty, equality and fraternity?

When the revolutionaries in France took over control of the government from King Louis XVI, they wanted to make changes to improve life for ordinary people. Their slogan was: 'Liberty, Equality and **Fraternity**'. One of the first things they did was to pass a law setting out the rights of all citizens of France. This was called the Declaration of the Rights of Man. They then introduced some new laws.

Key points from the Declaration of the Rights of Man, 1789

All men are born free and equal.

All men have equal rights to freedom, property and security.

The law should be the same for everyone.

Every man is innocent until he is proved guilty.

No one should be uneasy about his opinions, even his religious beliefs.

Every citizen has freedom of speech.

 Which statement do you think is most important?
Which one could be omitted?
What impact would this have?

Did you know?

In 1793 a new calendar was introduced.

Years were counted from 22 September 1792 when the Revolutionary government was established. Weeks were ten days long, with every tenth day a day of rest. The traditional Sunday as a day of rest was abolished, as a way of reducing the influence of the Catholic Church in people's lives.

A notice of changes made by the Revolution

- Parliament rather than the king now makes the laws.

- Members of Parliament are elected by the people.

- All men aged over 25 who pay taxes are allowed to vote. Women are not allowed to vote.

- Criminals are to be tried by a jury of twelve men rather than by one judge.

- The most unpopular taxes have been stopped.

- Torture, branding and hanging are forbidden as punishments.

- Peasants are (for the first time) allowed to own land.

- The slave trade is abolished.

- Some Catholic churches are to be closed down because they have too much power and wealth. Their church lands to be sold to the peasantry.

- Lands owned by nobles are to be confiscated.

- Divorce is now legal.

Over to you ...

1 Working in pairs, decide whether these people below whether they would have been pleased or angry about the changes made by the Revolution, and why.

- A 26-year-old male peasant who pays taxes.

- A 45-year-old Catholic priest.

- A 20-year-old man arrested for robbery.

- A 30-year-old unhappily-married woman.

- A 29-year-old female slave.

The Terror

As time went by, the leaders of the Revolution became more worried about opposition and passed even stricter laws. Louis XVI was executed on 21 January 1793. His wife, Marie Antoinette, was executed on 16 October 1793. This was only the beginning of a huge number of executions in what became known as 'The Terror'. During this period more than 12,000 people from a total population of 28 million were executed and even more were imprisoned. Sometimes, just being suspected of not supporting the revolution was enough to get someone sent to the **guillotine**.

○ **Key words**

Guillotine
An instrument of execution where a sharp blade falls from a frame to cut off a person's head

(a)

■ *A drawing showing the deliberate drowning of 200 prisoners in December 1793. They were suspected of opposing the revolution and of being involved in a rebellion in Nantes.*

Did it work?

2 Look back at the Declaration of the Rights of Man. Which of the terms do you think were:

a) entirely achieved

b) partially achieved

c) Not achieved

In conclusion ...

3 Which of the statements below (**a–c**) do you agree with most and why?

a) The French Revolution largely introduced good changes, making France a better and fairer place. The Terror was necessary and only affected a tiny proportion of French people.

b) The French Revolution was a terrible period in French history. Those that suffered outweighed those that benefited from the Revolution.

c) The French Revolution brought about benefits for ordinary people, but the suffering of the clergy, nobles and opponents of the Revolution was great.

Back to the start

In Lessons 1.5a to 1.5d you have studied the American Revolution and the French Revolution. There were many similarities between these two revolutions. How were they similar? Think about:

● the cause of the revolutions

● who governed the countries

● the ways in which life improved

● the ways in which life did not improve.

What are the differences (if any)?

Do you think it was a coincidence that both revolutions happened so close together?

1.5e

Taking it further!

Key words

Plantations
Large farms growing sugar or cotton often requiring the use of slave labour.

❓ **What clues does source a give you about the kind of person Toussaint might have been?**

■ *Toussaint showed no mercy towards his enemies, as this French engraving of French soldiers being executed in 1805 shows. On another occasion, Toussaint ordered his troops to burn food stores and homes, and poison wells to defeat the enemy.*

Toussaint L'Ouverture: Hero of Haiti?

In the eighteenth century, the small Caribbean island of San Domingo (now Haiti and the Dominican Republic) was ruled by France. The French made great profits from the sale of the sugar that was grown on the island, and forced black slaves to work on the **plantations**. The slaves had no freedom. They had to work long hours and were treated cruelly.

When news reached San Domingo that revolution in France had been successful, the slaves hoped that the new government of France would give them liberty and equality too. With this in mind they launched a rebellion against their white owners on the island in August 1791.

The slaves were led by the former slave Toussaint L'Ouverture. He has been presented as a brave and fair leader: the hero of Haiti. But can these accounts be believed?

a

■ *Toussaint L'Ouverture painted by an anonymyous artist in 1805.*

b
Toussaint alone among the black leaders organised thousands of untrained blacks into an army capable of fighting European troops. It is characteristic of him that he began with a few hundred picked men, loyal to him. In camp he drilled and trained them thoroughly.

■ *Written by C. L .R. James in his book The Black Jacobins, 1938.*

c
His first care was to establish religion and to encourage the industry of those who were under his control. Such was the progress of agriculture, that the next harvest produced (despite the destruction caused by nearly ten years of war) one-third of the quantity of sugar and coffee that had been produced during Haiti's most prosperous period.

■ *From an account by Marcus Rainsford from 1805.*

d

e
Toussaint lined up the rebels and decided who should be shot. He introduced a passport system to stop people moving freely about the island without permission. Anyone encouraging disorder could be condemned to six months' hard labour with a weight attached to his foot by a chain.

■ *Written by C. L .R. James in 1989.*

f

All Toussaint's actions were made to increase his own power. He spent huge amounts on building grand houses, and in two years these black chiefs became the richest private individuals in the world.

■ *Written by John Brown in 1837.*

g

He says a thousand rosaries (prayers) a day in order to deceive everyone the better.

■ *Written by Georges Biassou sometime before his death in 1807*

h

- There cannot exist slaves on this territory. All men are born, live and die free.
- All men, regardless of colour, should be given employment.
- The law is the same for all people regardless of colour.

■ *Some of the laws passed for Haiti by Toussaint in 1801.*

Who wrote about Toussaint?

C.L.R. James:	Marcus Rainsford:	Georges Biassou:	John Brown:
a historian born in Trinidad in 1901. He admired the slaves of Haiti for having led the first successful slave revolt in history, but he tries to write an objective account that looks at both sides.	a white British author who was in favour of ending the slave trade in Britain in 1806. He was writing at the time of the Haitian revolution.	a former slave and leader of the slave revolt on Haiti. He fell out with Toussaint after losing power to him. He also disagreed with Toussaint's lenient treatment of white former slave owners.	a white American who argued against slavery.

What can we learn about Toussaint L'Ouverture?

1 Use **sources b–h** to find out more about Toussaint. Was he a brave and fair leader? Watch out though! You need to think carefully about each of the sources. For each source, make a note of the following:

- What it says. (Does it give you a positive or negative view of Toussaint?)
- Who wrote it.
- Why they wrote it.

Use the information about the authors above to help you with the last two points.

2 Now look at the three claims below. Based on **sources b–h** do you:

- agree with each claim
- disagree with each claim
- neither agree nor disagree with each claim?

Make sure you can explain your point of view.

Claim 1: Toussaint was an effective military leader.

Claim 2: Toussaint was selfish and deceitful and only wanted power and wealth.

Claim 3: Toussaint was a good ruler of Haiti.

Next Lesson

In this lesson you will:

- find out why the Gordon Riots started, and what the impact was on London

- investigate why a street protest became a riot.

Key words

Riot

A public act of violence by a mob.

Riot Act

Act that allowed the local authorities to force a group of twelve or more people to leave a place that they were gathered or face the consequences.

The Gordon Riots of 1780

It's human nature to get upset about things that don't go the way you want them to. You might be angry enough to show your frustration to others, but when would you join a mob of people to destroy property in a **riot**?

- The Poll Tax Riots took place in London on 31 March 1990. These riots were public protests against a tax introduced by the government at the time.

(?) *Why do people protest? In pairs come up with a list of things which people protest about by going on a demonstration. Compare your list with that of another pair.*

Why the riots happened

In the summer of 1780 a riot happened in London that lasted for five days. It was a surprise to the government and to many people who lived in the city. Look at the boxed information below about the build-up to the riot.

The Protestant Association collected a petition of 60,000 names to present to Parliament during a demonstration on 2 June 1780.

Lord George Gordon believed that being Catholic made you a traitor to the country. His group, called 'The Protestant Association', wanted the government to get rid of the new laws that helped Catholics.

The demonstration to Parliament got out of hand, and people started to attack known Catholic's houses and property.

In 1778 Britain was fighting wars against France, Spain and America, and needed more soldiers. All soldiers had to make a promise to fight for the king and the Protestant Church of England. But many Catholics felt they could not do this.

The government passed laws that helped Catholics by saying Catholic soldiers did not have to promise loyalty to the Church of England.

Your turn ...

1 Try to work out why the riots happened. Look at the events that happened before the riot. Use the clues in the text to list these events in the correct chronological order (from 1 to 5). Use a table like the one here.

Event	Order number

How people reacted

The Gordon Riots were a shock to many people at the time. London had no organised police force, and the army could only come on to the streets if the **Riot Act**, which was a warning to the mob, had been read out loud. Once it had been read out, soldiers still had to wait 20 minutes before acting.

The riots took place all over London and many people were caught up in the events that were happening around them. One eyewitness of the Gordon Riots was Susan Burney, the daughter of a music historian who lived near Westminster in London and wrote several letters to her sister describing what she saw.

5 June, 1780

William came into the living room looking alarmed saying there was terrible rioting on the streets and that the mob were breaking several windows and threatening to set fire to some of the houses because Roman Catholics lived in them. The evening before they had burned down a chapel in Moor Fields and several Catholic's houses.

5 June, 1780

The mob broke in to Sir George Saville's House and took out his furniture. They piled it up in the square, then they forced Sir George's servant to bring them a candle to set fire to it.

6 June, 1780

We saw the mob throw chairs, tables, clothes – everything the house contained. And because there was too much furniture for one fire, they made several. At one time I counted six of these fires.

Did you know?

One of the prisons that burned down in the riot was called 'The Clink'. It was never rebuilt, but people still use the name as slang for being in prison.

Popery
An old and insulting term for Roman Catholicism.

Treason
A crime against the government of a country.

6 June, 1780

In the middle of these events Miss Kirwan arrived terrified to death, then my sister. Each got to our door through the crowd with difficulty. They returned home more dead than alive.

6 June, 1780

When Hyde's house was emptied of all its furniture, the mob tore away the windows and window frames. Then they began to pull up the floors and the panels of the rooms, till some of the Protestant neighbours pleaded with the rioters not to keep up so strong a fire before their houses.

7 June, 1780

This was more alarming than any thing – for if the military power would not act, the rioters did not fear them.

7 June, 1780

*While Mr B, my sister and I stood at the window, the crowd grew smaller, as the mob had flown to attack other places. I saw about ten men and women in a group looking up at our windows. 'No **Popery**', they cried. They repeated this two or three times.*

Write a brief description

2 Imagine you are a reporter for a newspaper in 1780. Write a brief description of the riots using no more than 100 words. Use Susan Burney's letters to explain to people outside of London the events of June 1780.

■ *An engraving of Newgate Prison burning down during the Gordon Riots of 1780, published that year.*

Prisons

During the Gordon Riots, several prisons were attacked – including Newgate Prison, which was hated by the common people. It was almost destroyed, and prisoners were released by the mob.

The cost of the riots

After four days of violence, the Riot Act was read by the authorities. This allowed the military to act to calm the situation. Nonetheless, the damage to property was great. More than 100 buildings connected to the Catholic Church had been attacked and damage caused to the value of £30,000 (the equivalent to £3 million today). The buildings included Catholic churches in the capital and even the house of the former prime minister, Lord Rockingham. However, by the end of five days of rioting there had been 139 arrests, with 285 rioters killed and a further 173 wounded.

At the end of the riot, Lord George Gordon was put on trial for **treason**. This was the worst crime anyone could commit, and if he had been found guilty he would have been executed. However, he was found not guilty and went free.

Give explanations

3 Do you think that Lord George Gordon really wanted to start a riot?

a) Make two lists:

● one that records the main events of the protest

● one that identifies the causes of the protest.

b) Using a Venn diagram, link the causes (in red) with the events (in black), to identify reasons why the protest became a riot.

c) Compare your answers with another member of your group. Which of the reasons you have identified was the most important and why?

4 What do you think might have stopped the protest becoming a riot?

1.6b

In this lesson you will:

- find out what happened at the Peterloo Massacre

- show how a historical event can be interpreted in different ways.

What was the Peterloo Massacre, 1819?

When historians write about the past, they will often express their opinions – what they think. People writing or drawing at the time of an event will also express their opinions. Sometimes, when opinions differ, it is difficult for historians to work out what is true (or fact) and what is not.

? *Think about someone from the past – perhaps Queen Elizabeth I or William the Conqueror. Note down five words you think describe what type of person they were. What did others in your class write? What reasons are there for the differences?*

Manchester 1819

I fought for my country at the Battle of Waterloo in 1815, which finally brought the wars against the French to an end. I saw thousands of men killed and was lucky to survive myself.

But when we soldiers came home we found high bread prices and even higher unemployment. We aren't able to let our feelings be known, as only the rich are allowed to vote for Members of Parliament. I think that if working people could elect MPs they would pass laws to help us.

As **source a** shows, demands for the vote came to a head in August 1819, when a meeting was called in St Peter's Field in Manchester to hear local campaigners. What happened next became known as 'Peterloo'.

'The Massacre at Peterloo', a cartoon from 1819 by George Cruikshank.

Look and think

1 Look at **source a**. If you were using this painting as a source for a description of the event, what five questions would you want to ask the artist about his work?

A huge crowd had gathered to hear the speakers. Among them was Henry Hunt, a popular figure with the working classes because of his demands for the vote for ordinary people. At the edge of the field were the local **yeomanry**, mounted on horses and armed with swords. There are many reports about what happened next, as **sources b–d** show.

b

It seemed to be a festival day with the country people who were mostly dressed in their best and brought with them their wives, and I saw boys and girls taking their fathers' hands in the procession. At length Hunt made his appearance. On reaching the stage he was received with enthusiastic applause. I heard the sound of a horn, and immediately the Manchester Yeomanry appeared. They galloped towards the stage. Their **sabres** glistened in the air, and on they went. As the cavalry approached the people, they tried to escape, but so closely were they pressed together that immediate escape was impossible.

■ *Eyewitness account from John Smith, a moderate reformer.*

c

When Hunt and his friends had taken their station on the stage, it is supposed that no fewer than 150,000 people were gathered in the area near St Peter's Church. Hunt proceeded to speak to the huge crowd. While speaking, and without any sign of disorder occurring, our fears were raised to horror by the appearance of the Manchester Yeomanry, who were galloping into the area, ready for action. The bugle sounded a charge, and a scene of murder and bloodshed followed. Men, women and children of all ages became the victims of these monsters. People flew in every direction to avoid these hair-brained assassins.

■ *Eyewitness account from John Saxton, a radical reformer probably involved in writing the article that appeared in The Manchester Observer on 21 August 1819.*

d

Early in the afternoon, local magistrates called the cavalry to arrest two persons, Hunt and Johnson, who were on the stage. The infantry was ready, but I was determined not to bring them into contact with the people, unless necessary; not a shot has been fired by the people against the troops. I have, however, great regret in stating that some of the unfortunate people who attended this meeting have suffered from sabre wounds, and many from the pressure of the crowd. One of the Manchester Yeomanry, if not dead, lies without hope of recovery. It is understood he was struck with a stone. One of the special constables has been killed.

■ *Eyewitness account from Lieutenant-Colonel George L'Estrange, Commander of the Yeomanry at St Peter's Field.*

Key words

Home Secretary

The government minister responsible for the security of the country.

Sabres

Curved swords used by the cavalry.

Yeomanry

A local volunteer defence force, made up of soldiers on horseback.

Tell it as it was

7 Imagine you are a reporter on a local Manchester newspaper that usually supports the government. You have been given three eyewitness accounts (**sources b–d**) of the protest at St Peter's Field.

a) Write a brief but convincing 100-word outline of what you think really happened that day.

b) Using the same sources, what differences would you expect to see in a report published in a newspaper that supported the protesters?

■ 'Manchester Heroes': this cartoon of the Peterloo Massacre was published in 1819.

Linking it together

3 News travelled slowly at the beginning of the nineteenth century, but acting as an adviser for the government, you have been asked to inform the **Home Secretary** about what happened in St Peter's Field. The information is confused, and you must sort it out.

a) First, you receive the cartoon in **source e**. Based on this alone, what sort of advice would you give to the Home Secretary about the nature of the disturbances? How do you help him to distinguish between fact and opinion?

b) Then you receive **sources a–d**. Rank these sources according to how believable you think they are. In what ways does this change your views and why?

Back to the start

Imagine you lived through both the Gordon Riots and the Peterloo Massacre. You have been asked for your opinion about the following two viewpoints. Which would you agree with and why?

Viewpoint 1: It is the first responsibility of any government to keep the people of the country safe.

Viewpoint 2: In Britain, the people have a right to protest against things they believe to be wrong.

Next Lesson

1.6c

Taking it further!

The Cato Street conspiracy

In 1820 unemployment, hunger and revolutionary ideas swept across Britain.

Courier
11 killed at 'Peterloo'!

The Observer
Napoleon defeated!

New Times
New laws rise bread prices

The Post
No job for soldiers!

And Mr Edwards here has a proposal for our group.

George Edwards, a government spy, had joined Arthur Thistlewood's radical group who were planning an armed uprising.

Here's our chance to overthrow the government. We can attack the house and kill them all…

Edwards suggested that the group should attack several government ministers to cause unrest. However the plan had been made up by the government themselves and there was no dinner.

Ministers dine together

Thistlewood hoped that their actions would be the spark that would cause the people to rise up and overthrow the government.

What's the plan?

Look at the first four frames of the story.

1 What reasons can you find that might explain why there would be a plot against the Government?

2 How did the plotters hope to be successful?

3 What were they hoping would happen as a result?

Edwards revealed Thistlewood's plans to his boss and told them where they would be meeting up just before the attack.

The group were meeting in a stable in Cato Street. The government now knew all about the plan and set men to watch as the group gathered.

We are peace officers. Lay down your arms!

The police officers decided to make their move and went to arrest Thistlewood and his group. The arrests were made, but during the scuffle one of the police officers was killed.

At the trial of the group Edwards was nowhere to be seen and he did not testify. Despite this almost all were found guilty of High Treason.

You shall be hanged by the neck until dead.

Thistlewood and ten other conspirators were hanged, drawn and quartered on 1st May 1820. They were the last people to be punished in this way in Britain.

Point of view

Using the images on these pages, complete a diary that records the events surrounding the conspiracy from George Edwards' point of view. In it try and explain why you feel that the actions were being taken and what your role is.

Both sides of the story

Was the Government right to use the methods that it did to find and punish the plotters in the way that it did?

Imagine that you were able to conduct two separate interviews, one with a Government minister of the time and one with a family member of the gang.

Before you ask your questions, look back at what happened before the events of Cato Street and consider how this might influence the replies that each person would give to your questions.

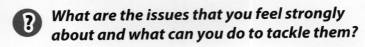

In this lesson you will:

- find out why people supported the movement known as Chartism

- try to link causes.

Why did people become Chartists?

Everybody has a point of view and most people have something that they feel strongly about, such as the environment or smoking.

? *What are the issues that you feel strongly about and what can you do to tackle them?*

The Charter

Many people in the 1830s felt very strongly about a number of issues. Indeed, they were so angry they decided to draw up a charter – a list of their demands. The first charter was written by William Lovett in 1838. It had six main points.

What are the problems?

1 Below are the complaints of people who have become Chartists. The years are 1837 and 1838. Read through each one and, in your own words, explain each complaint on a spider diagram.

I am a stocking weaver from Nottingham. But no one seems to be buying stockings at the moment and I have been out of work for two months. You have to be rich to be a Member of Parliament (MP) because they do not get paid. We want a 'People's Parliament' with MPs from all walks of life. This would mean that, from now on, MPs should be paid.

I come from Tregawny in Cornwall. Some of the people in our village have the vote. The problem is that to vote they have to go to the market square and put their hands up to support one of the candidates. Our landlord thinks he should decide who should be the MP and he watches to see who his tenants vote for. If he thinks they vote the wrong way, he throws them out of their houses. I think that everyone should be able to vote in secret.

■ *A painting from 1755 by William Hogarth showing voting during an election.*

Last summer the harvest was bad and the price of bread is high. I have not worked for months. I fear having to take my family into the dreaded workhouse. Parliament does not care about people like me; the workhouses are prisons for the poor. I want every man in the country over the age of 21 to have the vote. That will stop Parliament introducing laws that penalise the poor.

I am a printer in London. I want to become an MP but I can't because I do not own any property. This is not fair. People should be able to become an MP even if they do not own property.

I live and work in Birmingham. In 1832 we demanded that we were given our own MPs and the Reform Act in 1832 gave us two. We should have more because there are around 100,000 people living in Birmingham. There is a place in Suffolk called Eye which has one MP and a population of only 2,000. This is unfair and ridiculous. We think that constituencies should be the same size.

Parliament does not pass laws to help the working people. In 1833 it passed a Factory Act, but that did not protect factory children as much as it should have. We can stop Parliament making bad decisions by having an election every year.

What should be done?

2 Imagine you are the Chartist leader William Lovett. You are in the process of drawing up your Charter. You have decided to make six points. Each point will be explained. Here is an example:

We want there to be an election every year because we think that this will make Parliament pass laws that help everyone.

What are your other five points?

In conclusion ...

3 Working in pairs, imagine that you are Chartists. You are going to present your campaign to the outside world.

● One of you is going to explain what you, as Chartists, want.

● The other should explain what you think the result of a successful Charter would be.

Discuss your ideas before presenting them.

History detective

The Chartists were not the only people to campaign against something they did not like in Great Britain. Find out more about one of the following two protest groups.

● Anti-Corn Law League.

● Luddites.

Chartism: the ups and downs

All Chartists had one aim: to achieve the Charter (see opposite). The question was how they would achieve this! **Source a** is an engraving of the Newport Rising in 1839.

■ An engraving of the Newport Rising, November 1839.

The six points of the People's Charter

1 Every man over 21 who is not a criminal or insane should be allowed to vote.

2 Voting should be done in secret.

3 You do not have to be rich or own property to become an MP.

4 All MPs should be paid for doing their job.

5 All voting areas should be the same size.

6 Elections should be held every year.

? *What tactics does source a suggest the Chartists used?*

Highs and lows of Chartist

Between 1837 and 1848 the Chartists used a number of tactics to try to achieve the Charter. They also experienced some high and many low points.

Put them in order...

1 You are about to plot some of the Chartists' highs and lows onto a graph. To help you, read through nine of the most important events of Chartism.

   a) Put the events in date order on a timeline along the horizontal axis of your graph.

b) Now plot each event onto your graph using these scores:

   3 to 5: brilliant success for the Chartists

   1 to 2: positive development for the Chartists

   0: neither side wins

   -1 to -2: a defeat for the Chartists

   -3 to -5: a disastrous defeat for the Chartists

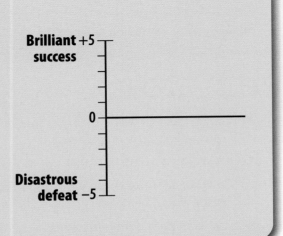

November 1837: Newspaper

Chartist leader Feargus O'Connor set up the *Northern Star* newspaper to spread Chartist ideas. By 1840, the newspaper had a circulation of 40,000, but hundreds of thousands of people would have known what was in its pages because newspapers were read out at meetings.

February 1839: National Convention

The Chartist Convention met to discuss the first Petition and Charter. These were exciting times.

May 1839: Meeting

Thousands of Chartists attended an open air meeting at Kersal Moor, addressed by the Chartist leader Feargus O'Connor. The meeting was a great success.

July 1839: The Bull Ring Riot

Clashes between the police and Chartists in Birmingham led to rioting and the troops were called out. The riot was crushed, and Chartist leaders William Lovett and John Collins were arrested and imprisoned.

November 1839: Uprising

A crowd of 7,000 Chartists marched into the town of Newport and attacked the Westgate Hotel defended by soldiers. The uprising failed. A number of Chartisted leaders, including William Lovett and Feargus O'Connor, were arrested. Many Chartists were deported to Australia.

May 1842: Second petition

Three and a half million people signed the second Chartist petition. It was rejected by Parliament by 287 to 47 votes.

August 1842: Plug Riots

A number of Chartists become involved in strikes known as the Plug Riots. The strikers pulled the plugs out of steam machines. They also rioted in a number of northern towns including Preston.

April 1845: Land Society

The Chartist movement approved the idea of their leader, Feargus O'Connor, and set up the Chartist Land Society with the aim of encouraging working people to settle on the land.

April 1848: Third petition

More than 50,000 Chartists met on Kennington Common. The Queen was so frightened that she left London. But the petition was rejected by Parliament and Chartism faded away.

Sometimes the Chartists used violence to try to 'persuade' people to accept the Charter. Other times they used peaceful means.

Which was the more effective?

2   Look again at the boxes.

   a) Which are examples of violent methods of trying to get the Charter?

   b) Which are examples of peaceful methods?

   c) In your opinion, which were the most successful methods for the Chartists: violent or peaceful methods?

In conclusion ...

3   In no more than 250 words, explain what the Chartists wanted and how they tried to achieve their aims.

Back to the start

In 1848 the Third Charter was rejected. However, by 1900 five out of the six points of the Charter had been achieved. Does this mean that Chartism was a success or a failure?

1.7c

Taking it further!

Who was Lydia Becker?

The Chartists argued for the vote for all men over 21, but who did they leave out? Some women thought that women should be given the vote too. One such woman was Lydia Becker. In 1866 she got together with some friends to set up Manchester Women's Suffrage Committee to campaign for votes for women. In 1870 she set up the *Women's Suffrage Journal* and in 1887 Becker was elected president of the National Union of Women's Suffrage Societies (NUWSS).

■ *Lydia Becker.*

Read about Lydia in **sources a–e**. As you read, think about two questions:

- What were Lydia's main ideas?
- What methods did she use?

a The shortest and most effective way, nay, the only way, of raising the position of women, is to give them votes.

■ *From a letter written by Lydia Becker to Josephine Butler, November 1868.*

b

WOMEN'S SUFFRAGE.
THE BRISTOL AND WEST OF ENGLAND SOCIETY.
A PUBLIC MEETING
IN CONNECTION WITH THIS SOCIETY WILL BE HELD AT THE
ROYAL PUBLIC ROOMS, EXETER,
On TUESDAY, APRIL 14th, 1874.
RESERVED SEAT TICKET.
Miss BEEDY, M.A.,
Miss GARRET, (of London,)
Miss L. S. ASHWORTH, (of Bath,)
And several Local Gentlemen are expected to take part in the Meeting.
Doors open at 7 p.m., to commence at 7.30.
EXETER, 7th April, 1874.   F. TOWNSEND, Hon. Sec. Exeter Branch.

c It is a great mistake to suppose that domestic duties are limited to girls and women. Every boy in Manchester should be taught to darn his socks and cook his own chops.

■ *From Lydia Becker's scrapbook, February 1877.*

■ *Ticket for a Woman's Suffrage Meeting, 1880.*

d Lydia's work had lasting results. The editor of the *Manchester Guardian* newspaper thought that Lydia was responsible for bringing women successfully into the area of public speaking. She changed the public's attitude towards women speaking.

■ *Adapted from an article by the historian Joan Parker 2001.*

e Women are a force which, if gathered together, led, organised and visible, will lead us women to victory.

■ *Lydia Becker, 1880.*

Draw conclusions ...

1 Answer the two questions at the start of this topic:

● What were Lydia's main ideas?

● What methods did she use?

Use evidence from **sources a–e** to support your answers.

2 What do you think of Lydia Becker? Write three sentences beginning like the one below, using 'because' in the middle:

I think Lydia Becker was ....

because ....

3 Now compare your three sentences with those written by someone else in your class. Do you both share the same opinion of Becker? Can you think of reasons for any agreement or disagreement?

History detective

This is your chance to be a history detective! Find out more about nineteenth-century women who wanted women to have the vote. Your investigation should look into two things:

● the methods that nineteenth-century women used to promote votes for women

● other issues that they were involved in such as education.

Go to www.heinemann.co.uk/hotlinks for a website that provides a good starting point. But watch out! There are some women on this list who lived into the twentieth century; your task is to find out about women who died before 1901.

Back to the start

Look back over the last three lessons. How did Lydia Becker's tactics differ from those of the Chartists?

Next Lesson

How did who held power change from 1603 to 1901?

In this unit you have explored how much power the rulers of Britain had, and how far their powers changed during the period 1603 to 1901.

Think back to your work at the beginning of the Unit when the monarch held most of the power. By 1901 things had changed and Parliament was in control. The amount of power ordinary people had also changed, as more and more people were allowed to vote to choose the government.

Your task is to find out how these changes happen and which key events affected the shift of power.

Your turn ...

1 Use a graph like the one below and choose 5 or 6 events that you have studied and that you think changed who held the power in Britain. Add these events to the timeline at the bottom of the graph.

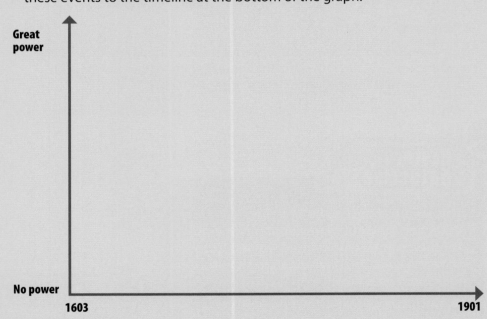

You are going to plot on the graph how each event affected how much power the following had:

- the monarch
- Parliament
- middle- and working-class men
- middle- and working-class women.

Remember that not all these groups might be affected by each event.

Your turn ...

2 Draw onto your own copy of the graph a cross for each event to show how much power the monarch had. Now join up these crosses.

Now draw crosses onto your graph to show the power of Parliament at each event and use another colour to join these up. Next take another colour and do the same for middle- and working-class men, and then a fourth colour for middle- and working class-women.

3 When you have completed your graph, compare your line with a partner. Discuss in pairs what you notice about your lines and what this tells you about how the balance of power shifted between 1603 and 1901.

Your turn ...

4 Based on your completed graph, discuss each statement below in pairs and decide if you agree, disagree or partially agree with it.

- The power of the monarch decreased in the period 1603 to 1901 as the power of Parliament increased.

- It was impossible for the monarch and Parliament to cooperate and share power.

- The Civil War was the most important event in shifting the balance of power between the monarch and the king.

- Middle- and working-class people were only able to gain power through acts of violence.

Write down your conclusions and remember to back up your verdict with reasons.

Charles I: martyr or tyrant?
Why has Charles I been remembered in different ways?

This task focuses on the skill of interpretation. It is the job of the historian to:

- show how opinions or interpretations differ
- explain why they differ.

You are going to read three different people's interpretations of Charles I and suggest reasons for them.

■ *John Bradshaw's view of Charles I at Charles' trial in January 1649. John Bradshaw was the judge at the trial. He was chosen for this role by Parliament.*

a Charles I is a tyrant, traitor, murderer and public enemy to the good of this nation. He out of a wicked design to uphold his own power, tried to overthrow the rights and liberties of the people of England. He shall therefore be put to death by severing of his head from his body.

■ *The front cover of the* Eikon Basilike, *a collection of the private views and prayers of Charles in the last months of his life, published just after his death in 1649. The* Eikon Basilike *was probably put together by John Gauden, Bishop of Worcester, who sympathised with Charles. In 1660, after Charles II had been returned to the throne, the Church of England made Charles I a saint, and ordered that the date of his death, 30 January, be a day of special religious remembrance.*

■ *Charles Dickens' view of Charles I, from A Child's History of England, written in 1854. Dickens wrote this book during the reign of Queen Victoria. By this time, it was Parliament and not the monarch who had most power and this was felt to be correct. Indeed, Queen Victoria removed 30 January as a day of special celebration for Charles I from the Church calendar.*

c Now, you are to understand that King Charles the First – of his own determination to be a high and mighty King …deliberately set himself to put his Parliament down and to put himself up. You are also to understand, that even in pursuit of this wrong idea (enough in itself to have ruined any king) he never took a straight course, but always took a crooked one and was always remarkably unforgiving. Charles … seized upon his subjects' goods and money at his pleasure, and punished according to his … will all who ventured to oppose him.

1 Look at each source in turn. For each source, write down what impression it gives you of Charles I.

2 How does the impression given of Charles I in **source b** differ from that of **source c**?

3 Why do **sources a, b** and **c** give different impressions of Charles I?

4 Give two reasons why **sources b** and **c** differ in their interpretation of Charles.

How are you going to set about a task like this?

Question 1

This question is quite straightforward. The sources provide a lot of information about Charles I. When answering this question make sure that you do the following:

- make at least three points about Charles I for each source
- make the points in your own words, rather than just copying what the source says
- back up each main point with a short quote from the source. Here is an example from **source a**:

Charles I was cruel and did not care about his people because it says he was 'a murderer ...who tried to overthrow the rights and liberties of the people.'

Question 2

This question asks you to compare two sources and describe how they give different views of Charles. When putting together your answer think about the following.

- Is Charles shown as arrogant and power hungry?
- Is Charles shown as religious and caring?
- Is Charles shown as a victim or as guilty?

Try to back up each main point with a short quote or a description of the source if it is a picture.

Question 3

Remember the 5Ws! (See page 182 if you need a reminder.) In particular, think about who wrote each source and when they were writing to explain their differing views.

Question 4

This question follows on from 3. In answering question 3 you should have given some general reasons why the sources differ. Now use these ideas to explain why these two sources differ.

How will your work be marked? Have you:

Level 4
Described some different interpretations of the past?

Identified and used some information from the two sources as examples to back up your points?

Produced work which shows some structure?

Level 5
Suggested some reasons for different interpretations of the past?

Selected and used information from the sources as examples to back up your points?

Produced work which is carefully structured?

Level 6
Explained how and why different interpretations of the past have arisen or been constructed?

Selected and used relevant information from the sources as examples to back up your points?

Produced work which is carefully and clearly structured?

Assessment 2

Was revolution the road to freedom? How much changed as a result of the revolutions in England, America and France?

In this unit you have explored revolution in three countries: Britain, America and France. There are similarities between the revolutions which all aimed to bring greater freedom to ordinary people. But did each revolution bring about that much change?

1 For each of the revolutions you have studied in this Unit complete a table like the one below. Use what you have previously learned about each revolution to help you.

	England	America	France
Who held most power before?			
Who/what held most power afterwards?			
Peaceful or violent?			
Afterwards could a wealthy man who owned property vote?			
Could a poor man vote?			
Could a woman vote?			
Were any groups discriminated against after the revolution?			
Were all religions respected equally afterwards?			
Did people have more/fewer rights and freedoms afterwards?			

2 Once you have completed the table, work in pairs to compare the results of the revolutions to make a judgement about the following:

- Which revolution brought about the fewest political changes?

- Did all the revolutions give ordinary people a greater say in who held power over them?

- Did ordinary people suffer in the way each revolution was brought about?

- After which revolution did people continue to be discriminated against the most?

- After which revolution did the rights of ordinary people improve the least?

Use evidence from your table to back up your answers.

3 How much changed as a result of the revolutions in England, America and France? Choose one country and explain your answer.

How are you going to set about a task like this?

3 Plan your answer before you start and remember to explain:

- why people in your chosen country felt they were ruled unfairly before the revolution

- how, after the revolution, the government was designed to be fairer

- how the new government aimed to bring more freedom and better rights for the people

- how not everyone benefited from the change in government.

Remember to add a conclusion at the end. This should explain your own view about how much changed as a result of the revolution.

How will your work be marked?
Have you:

Level 4
Described some some of the changes brought about by the revolutions?

Identified and used some information as examples to show some of the changes brought about by the revolutions?

Produced work which shows some structure?

Level 5
Described some of the changes brought about by the revolutions?

Selected and used information as examples to show some of the changes brought about by the revolutions?

Used proper historical terms?

Level 6
Explained the extent of change brought about by each revolution?

Selected and used relevant information as examples to show the extent of changes brought about by the revolutions?

Used proper historical terms?

Produced work that is carefully and clearly structured into paragraphs?

Attempted to explain your judgement about which revolution was most successful?

Unit 2
Living and working

What was England like in 1603?

Look at this picture.

? *Make a note of three things that surprise you most about England in 1603.*

? *Now note down three things that you would have liked the least about life in 1603.*

Medicine and health were very poor. Many babies died before their first birthday.

There were not many good roads and most people did not leave the village where they were born. The only really big city was London.

People who were not farmers often worked from their own home, for example making cloth from wool.

Timeline 1603–1901

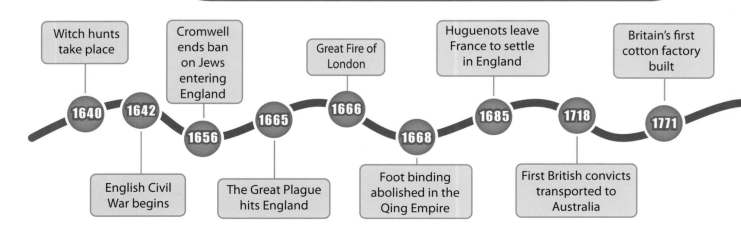

Witch hunts take place — 1640

Cromwell ends ban on Jews entering England — 1656

Great Fire of London — 1666

Huguenots leave France to settle in England — 1685

Britain's first cotton factory built — 1771

1642 — English Civil War begins

1665 — The Great Plague hits England

1668 — Foot binding abolished in the Qing Empire

1718 — First British convicts transported to Australia

The period that you are going to look at now, 1603–1901, was a time of great change for many people. You are going to find out about these changes, why they happened and what the country was like by 1901.

England's main industry in 1603 was farming, which had not changed much since medieval times. Each village grew most of the food that the people living there needed.

There was no official police force. If there was a problem, the government sent the army to that part of the country.

Water wheels were used to power buildings such as mills.

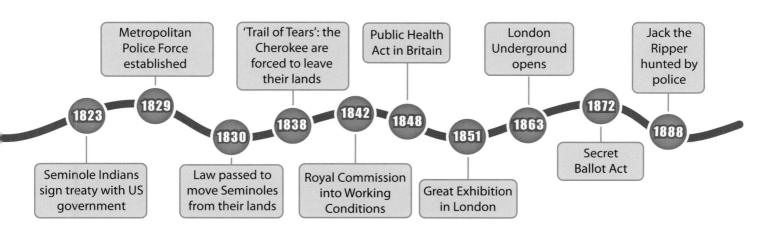

Metropolitan Police Force established

'Trail of Tears': the Cherokee are forced to leave their lands

Public Health Act in Britain

London Underground opens

Jack the Ripper hunted by police

1823 · 1829 · 1830 · 1838 · 1842 · 1848 · 1851 · 1863 · 1872 · 1888

Seminole Indians sign treaty with US government

Law passed to move Seminoles from their lands

Royal Commission into Working Conditions

Great Exhibition in London

Secret Ballot Act

What frightened people in the seventeenth century?

In this lesson you will:

- find out the how the Verney family lived and died

- weigh up how dangerous a threat disease was to people in the seventeenth century and why this was.

Deadly diseases

? *What are people frightened of today?*

Mary Blacknall married Sir Ralph Verney in 1629. Ralph was an MP, and owned several large houses and land in Buckinghamshire. But although Mary lived a very privileged life, she was not protected from the dangerous times she lived in: the English Civil War was fought in her lifetime and there was the constant threat of disease to her family's health.

1 Ralph Verney **married** Mary Blacknall **2**

3 Edmund
4 Mary
5 Anna Maria
6 Margaret
7 Jack
8 Ralph

Key:

1	Born 1613; died aged 83 possibly from stomach cancer.
2	Born 1616; died aged 34 possibly from tuberculosis.
3	Born 1636; died aged 52.
4	Born 1632; died soon after birth.
5	Born 1634; died aged 4.
6	Born 1639; died aged 8 of dysentery.
7	Born 1640; died aged 55. Married three times.
8	Born 1647; died aged 4 months.

Look and think

1 In pairs, look at the Verney family tree and answer these questions.

a) How many different causes of death are there?

b) How many of the Verney family died as children?

c) Does anything surprise you about the ages at which people died in Mary's family? Can you think of any explanations for why this might have been the case?

Doctors and treatments

When Mary Blacknall became ill, the doctor advised:

- giving her asses' milk mixed with herbs and spices
- that she should be bled by making a small cut under her tongue
- that leeches should be used to draw blood.

Remedies and cures

- Other remedies for illness in the seventeenth century included a recipe to: 'Take a ram's head, cut if off, boil it well, take out the brains, and put cinnamon, ginger and nutmeg inside it and heat them, stirring well.' The patient was to eat this with bread for fourteen days.
- When the plague struck, people carried nosegays (little bags of herbs and spices) to breath through because they believed the plague was caused by bad air. Some even wore dried toads around their necks, as charms to ward away the plague!

The Great Plague of 1665

Mary's son Jack fell ill with the plague while working in Turkey. He was one of the few who survived. In 1665 there was a serious outbreak of the plague in England. In London alone, 80,000 people died. Like many wealthy people, the Verneys left for the countryside to avoid the plague. Poorer Londoners were not allowed to leave the city without a certificate of good health, which explains why so many of them died.

■ This portrait of Mary Blacknall was painted during her lifetime.

Infant mortality

Mary's second child, also called Mary, died soon after birth. This was not uncommon at the time – about one in six babies died during the first year of their life.

Ignorance

- No one understood that germs cause disease. For example, people did not realise that a germ caused the plague or that it was spread by the fleas on black rats. Many people believed it was spread by cats and dogs. When the Lord Mayor offered a reward of two pence for every animal killed, 40,000 dogs and 200,000 cats died.
- Because people didn't know what caused disease, they did not know how to prevent or cure it. Instead, they blamed bad smells in the air or divine punishment. Some doctors believed illnesses were caused by a lack of balance of four liquids (which they called 'humours') in the body. They thought that draining blood from a patient would redress this imbalance.

Give some advice

2 Imagine you are a seventeenth-century doctor.
   You are to write a letter to one of your patients. In your letter you should advise:

   - what causes disease
   - how to avoid becoming ill.

Now try this

3 Write a good health guide for use by someone like Mary Verney. You should include:

   - information about the main threats to health in the seventeenth century
   - the causes of some of these illnesses.

   You should also suggest remedies and cures. (You could make up some of your own!)

In this lesson you will:

- investigate what happened during the witch hunts in the 1640s

- look at what caused people to make accusations of witchcraft.

Why were people accused of witchcraft?

In Essex and Suffolk in the 1640s as many as 300 women were arrested and interrogated. More than 100 were executed. The crime that these women were accused of was witchcraft. How was it possible that such a witch hunt could take place during the 1640s?
To begin with, look at **source a**.

■ *A woman under going the water test for witchcraft. The suspected witch was tied up and lowered into a river. From 1613.*

? *What can you see happening in this picture? Why do you think it is happening?*

Witches and their hunters

Imagine it is 1647 and you are living in Manningtree in Essex. Matthew Hopkins, the Witchfinder General, has just arrived in your area, determined to uncover any witches. Read the factfile on Hopkins to find out more about him. Then read Cases 1 and 2 about two local women who have been accused of witchcraft.

Factfile

Name: Matthew Hopkins **Address:** Lives in Essex
Work details: Began career as a witch finder in 1645.

Methods used:

- Strip search of accused to look for devil's marks.

- Keeps accused awake till they confess.

- The water test: ties the accused up and lowers into a river or pond. If she lives, she is guilty.

- Encourages local people to make accusations of witchcraft.

Payment:

- Fee paid for survey of possible witches.

- Fee to be paid for each witch found.

Case 1: Margaret Moone from Thorpe-le-Soken
Date: 1645

The people of Thorpe-le-Soken were not well off and had become poorer during the Civil War. A group of villagers accused Margaret Moone, a local elderly widow, of witchcraft.

Margaret was so poor that she received handouts to survive and had been forced to move out of her cottage. The villagers claimed that she then caused a neighbour to be covered suddenly by hundreds of lice, that she caused the death of cattle and horses, spoilt food and beer, and that she poisoned a local farmer and his family.

In 1645 Hopkins interrogated Margaret Moone who confessed to being a witch. At her trial she denied making a confession. She was convicted as a witch and hanged.

Case 2: Elizabeth Clarke from Manningtree
Date: 1645

Elizabeth Clarke was an elderly widow with one leg. She was so poor that she relied on handouts of money. Elizabeth's mother had been executed as a witch and so she had a reputation for witchcraft.

The people of Manningtree were becoming increasingly poor due to the disruption caused by Civil War, and by 1645 food and fuel were running short. A local man accused Elizabeth of causing two cows to die and of bewitching his wife with a terrible illness.

Matthew Hopkins interrogated Elizabeth Clarke, and after days of questioning she admitted that she was a witch. Hopkins took her to court. She was found guilty and hanged.

Be the lawyer

1 You have been asked to defend either Margaret Moone or Elizabeth Clarke at their witchcraft trial. However, you've got a head start because you've got Matthew Hopkins in the hot seat!

Choose which woman you are going to defend. Then make a list of questions you want to ask Hopkins about why he has accused this woman.

Prove the case

2 Some new evidence has just emerged (A–C). Select key points from this evidence to use in your defence.

Evidence A

An extract from *The Parliament Post*, newspaper from 1645, blamed the Royalists for an increase in witchcraft, saying: 'There is an increase in wickedness because the spirits of the Royalists have met with some of our women, and it has turned them into witches.'

Evidence B

John Gaule, the vicar of Huntingdonshire, explained the reasons why he did not want Matthew Hopkins to come near his parish, 1646: 'Every old woman with a wrinkled face, a furrowed brow, a hairy lip and a squint eye, a squeaking voice or a scolding tongue, will be called a witch.'

Evidence C

People did not understand what caused diseases. Life expectancy was short, and cattle plagues and other animal diseases were common but people did not know what caused these things. As the century progressed advances in science helped to explain the occurrence of disease and bad harvests.

Argue a case

3 You must write the speech that you will give to defend your chosen victim. In your speech make sure that you:

- undermine the people who accused her, including Hopkins himself
- attempt to explain why she confessed at first even though she is innocent
- explain why people might look to blame witches for their misfortunes.

Back to the start

Make a list of the dangers people faced in the seventeenth century. Compare your list with a partner and then rank each danger from 1–5 to show how serious you think it was.

2.1c

Taking it further!

Great Fire of London: accident or arson?

In the middle of the night, in a bakery on Pudding Lane in London on 2 September 1666, a spark ignited a fire which soon became a roaring firestorm. The fire's flames reddened the sky for four days and reached temperatures of over 1,000 degrees Celsius. The fire reduced the centre of London to ash, destroying more than 13,000 houses and 87 churches. Was the fire a terrible accident that spread quickly through the wooden buildings, or was it **arson**? Use the evidence to investigate the causes of the fire.

a

■ *The Great Fire of London, 1666, painted soon afterwards.*

A Thomas Farriner owned the bakery in Pudding Lane. He said that 'he had after 12 o'clock that night gone through every room and found no fire but one in the chimney, where the room was paved with bricks, this fire he diligently raked to **embers**'. He was sure the fire was started later on purpose.

B The bakery had a large oven, above which was stored chopped wood ready for the next day. All the houses were tightly packed together and were made of wood that was particularly dry from months of drought.

C On the night of 2 September there was a strong easterly wind. This may have blown a spark from the fire onto the chopped wood. The gale blew for four days, spreading the fire. Neighbours accused Thomas Farriner of returning home drunk.

D In a cellar further down Pudding Lane, twelve barrels of tar were stored which when heated by the fire exploded like a bomb.

E Men rushed to the church to collect buckets, but they found these either stolen or damaged. Basic fire engines arrived but were ineffective because at low tide there was not enough water in the pipes under the ground to operate the water jets. Firehooks (which were used to pull down buildings and stop fire by denying it the fuel to burn) were found, but the Lord Mayor of London told people not to use them because he did not want to pay compensation for the damage. The fire was halted four days later, partly because houses were pulled down.

F Rumours spread that fireballs were being thrown by foreigners and Catholics (England at the time was a mainly Protestant country) because some houses close to, but not directly next to, the flames caught fire. One witness said he saw 'a Frenchman in the act of firing a house in Shoe Lane'. At the time England was at war with France and Holland. England also feared attacks from Catholics.

G The Frenchman Robert Hubert was hanged in October 1666 for starting the fire. Hubert confessed that he came ashore in London on 2 September, went to the baker's house, placed a fireball on the end of a long pole and put it through a window. Hubert made many confessions, but all were slightly different and he was most probably tortured.

H Lawrence Petersen, a ship's captain, said that Robert Hubert had been a passenger on his ship. He remembered arriving in London and keeping Hubert in his cabin until 4 September 1666, when he escaped. Petersen said that Hubert had a weak mind, was mad, spoke no real English, and had a paralysed right leg and arm.

Key words

Arson
The crime of deliberately starting a fire.

Embers
The still hot, small pieces of wood left over after a fire.

What can we learn about the Great Fire?

1 Look at the statement below. Do you agree with it?

The fire was caused deliberately by foreign spies.

2 Give reasons to back up your opinion of this statement. Give examples to justify your view and explain why you think the opposite view is incorrect. Remember to organise your answer into clear sections.

Next Lesson

What was life like for immigrants in Britain?

In this lesson you will:

- discover the different skills that Jewish and Huguenot immigrants brought to England

- explore the impact of immigration on London's economy, society and industry.

Key words

Community

A group of people who live in a particular area.

Huguenots

French Protestants from the sixteenth and seventeenth centuries. They often suffered from oppression by the Catholic rulers of France.

Huguenot and Jewish immigrants

Source a is a photograph of the Jamme Masjid Mosque in East London. It was built as a church for **Huguenots**. This was later used by Methodists and, in the late nineteenth century, it became the Spitalfields Great Synagogue. Finally, it became the Jamme Masjid, or Great London Mosque, in 1976.

? *What does this building tell you about this area of London?*

- *The Jamme Masjid Mosque in East London.*

The East End of London saw great change throughout the seventeenth, eighteenth and nineteenth centuries – change that continues to this day. Many of these changes have been brought about by immigrant groups moving into the area. Two of the most important groups of immigrants were the Jews and Huguenots, but what impact did they have?

Factfile 1

Jewish immigrants

History

The Jewish **community** in London started to grow after Oliver Cromwell ended the ban on Jewish immigrants entering England in 1656. Over the next 200 years many Jewish families settled in London. Many Jewish people settled in the East End of London and by the late nineteenth century there was a growing Jewish community here.

Contribution to community

Mainly economic, e.g. they became market sellers, store owners, money lenders, fruit sellers and provided other essential services during the Industrial Revolution.

Popularity

Made a vital contribution to the growth of the British Empire but were not always liked, as some people resented the richer Jews their wealth.

Factfile 2

Huguenot immigrants

History

During the 1680s many French Protestants fled from France because they were badly treated by the Catholic Church. Many settled in the East End of London.

Contribution to community

Many Huguenots became silversmiths or brought their silk and watch-making skills to the British public.

These goods could be sold around the world. Many Huguenot families became involved in British banking and helped to further finance the British Empire.

Popularity

Welcomed into London life and quickly established themselves as hardworking members of the community.

Outline the impact

1 Using Factfiles 1 and 2, make a list of five positive impacts these immigrant communities had. Then, in pairs, discuss any reasons why some might have seen the arrival of these immigrants in a negative light.

Impact on the East End of London

Both the Jews and the Huguenots had an impact on the East End of London.

It soon became a centre of industry with many semi- and unskilled workers providing cheap labour.

There were many family businesses such as kosher butchers and silk-makers.

Communities were established that supported and cared for each other.

Local community groups published newspapers in their own languages.

They were allowed to worship in local synagogues and churches.

Housing was cheap and often badly built.

Many immigrants had been ill-treated in their own countries and so felt safer in London.

There were instances of racism, for example in 1888 'foreigners' were blamed for the Jack the Ripper murders.

Consider the information

2 a) Using the information in this lesson, copy and complete the table below.

Jewish contribution to society in eighteenth and nineteenth centuries	Huguenot contribution to society in eighteenth and nineteenth centuries

b) Now write a paragraph explaining which of these two groups you think made the biggest contribution to society in the eighteenth and nineteenth centuries. Use facts from your table to back up your answer.

Think again!

3 Imagine you are either a Huguenot or Jewish immigrant living in Britain during the nineteenth century. Write a letter to another member of your family encouraging them to come and live in London. In your letter you should:

- explain what skills will be useful for earning a living in Great Britain
- describe where they would be living in London
- describe the types of communities they would be living in
- explain how they will make money in their new country.

What was life like for immigrants in Britain?

Free black communities in Britain

All pictures can be used by a historian. They often give us a great deal of information. Look at **source a**.

? *What five things can you see in this picture? Make a list.*

■ *'A Milling Match', engraved by Thomas Rowlandson in 1811.*

Black communities in London

By the late eighteenth century there were large free black communities in Britain. Some of the black people living in Britain had served in the Royal Navy and Army. Others were ex-slaves who had gained their freedom then settled in Britain. The pictures shown in **sources b–d** give us a glimpse into the black community at the time.

Look carefully

1 Study **sources b–d**. Describe three points from each picture about the black community in Britain in the eighteenth and nineteenth centuries. You might want to describe:

● what the black people are doing

● where they are

● what other people around them are doing.

■ *An early-nineteenth-century picture showing a game of cards at a gentleman's club*

■ *Lowest 'Life in London' drawn by George Cruikshank in 1827.*

■ *Detail from a painting from the 1860's showing the death of Admiral Nelson in 1805.*

History detective

There were many black people who made a difference to British society. Find out about one of the following important people in British black history.

- William Cuffay
- Ira Aldridge
- Samuel Coleridge-Taylor
- Dr Ernest Goffe League

When writing your factfile, consider the following key points:

WHO?   **WHAT?**
WHERE?   **WHEN?**
WHY?   **HOW?**

Now write a Factfile about them.

Put information together

2 Explain what **sources b–d** tell us about the lives of black people in Britain in the eighteenth and nineteenth centuries. You might want to use the following sub headings to help you:

- work ● leisure ● lifestyle.

What impression do they give?

3 Artists and their work often show people's views at the time. Before we accept these sources as accurate we need to ask a few questions of each artist and picture.

- Is the image of black people in each picture positive, neutral or negative?
- What is the aim of each artist – show things as they were or to exaggerate for a reason?
- Overall, what is the attitude of the artists towards black people?

2.2c

Taking it further!

Mary Seacole and the Crimean War

During the 1850s Great Britain fought in the Crimean War against Russia. One of most lasting impressions of the Crimean War was the role that Florence Nightingale played in nursing wounded British soldiers. For many years historians wrote only about the improvements that she made to hospitals and nursing. They did not write about other important members of the British Empire who travelled to the Crimea to help soldiers.

Who was Mary Seacole?

■ *A portrait of Mary Seacole from 1869.*

Mary Seacole was born in 1805. She was the daughter of a Scottish soldier and a free black woman who ran a boarding house in Kingston, Jamaica.

Mary learned about medicine and herbal remedies from her mother. She used this knowledge to help cholera sufferers in 1850 when Kingston was hit by the disease. News of Mary's healing skills soon spread around the local area.

When Mary Seacole heard about the terrible hospital conditions and outbreaks of cholera in the Crimea she travelled to London. She wanted to join Florence Nightingale's nurses in the Crimea. Her application was rejected so she travelled to the war zone by herself.

When Mary arrived in the Crimea she went to a military hospital for soldiers located in Scutari. Once again, Florence Nightingale refused her offer of help.

Mary Seacole decided to open her own business to help the British soldiers. She called it the British Hotel, and sold fresh wholesome food and drinks to the soldiers. Mary then used the money she made to provide medical supplies and services to injured soldiers who needed her help. Florence Nightingale waited for soldiers to be brought to the hospital at Scutari, but Mary Seacole treated soldiers, including the enemy, on the battlefield. She just wanted to heal people. She continued to treat people in the Crimea until the war ended in 1856. However, Mary never became a qualified nurse and died in London in 1881.

What people wrote about Mary Seacole

Mary Seacole was often seen riding out to the front with baskets of medicines of her own preparation, and this is particularly the case after an engagement with the enemy.

■ *An article from* The Morning Advertiser, *19 January 1855.*

Using the knowledge she had acquired in the West Indies, Mary Seacole was able to give soldiers appropriate remedies for their ailments. But of much more importance, she was also able to charitably furnish them with proper nourishment, which they had no means of obtaining except in hospital. And most of that class had an objection to go into hospitals.

■ *Adapted from a letter written by Sir John Hall, Inspector-General of Hospitals, 30 June 1856.*

Here I met a celebrated person. A coloured woman, Mrs Seacole. Out of the goodness of her heart and at her own expense she supplied hot tea to the poor sufferers while they waited to be lifted into boats. She did not spare herself if she could do any good to the suffering soldiers.

■ *From a letter written by Doctor Reid (a surgeon in the British Army serving in the Crimea) to his family in 1855.*

Think it through

1 Imagine it is 1857 and you are a reporter for *The Times* newspaper. Your editor has asked you to interview a recent arrival in London called Mary Seacole. You have been told that she played an important role helping injured soldiers during the Crimean War. There will only be a small space in the newspaper for your article, so it must not be more than 300 words. Your editor says you must include:

- who Mary Seacole was
- who her parents were and where she was from
- how she developed her medical skills
- how she ended up in the Crimea
- what she achieved in the Crimea
- a quote about her work from another person
- your own personal opinion on the importance of her achievements.

Use all the sources in this lesson to help with your interview.

Was the Qing Dynasty educated, cultured and equal?

Qing Dynasty homes

Imagine a Chinese house so well built in the eighteenth century that it is still standing today. The only difference is it has moved hundreds of miles to be in America.

? *Can you find at least five features from the house below that are also in homes of today?*

On the move

Yin Yu Tang was the home of a Qing Dynasty merchant called Huang. He built the house in the village of Huang Cun near the mountains of Huangshan in southern China. In 1996 the remaining ancestors of the Huang family sold the house to the Essex Peabody Museum in the USA.

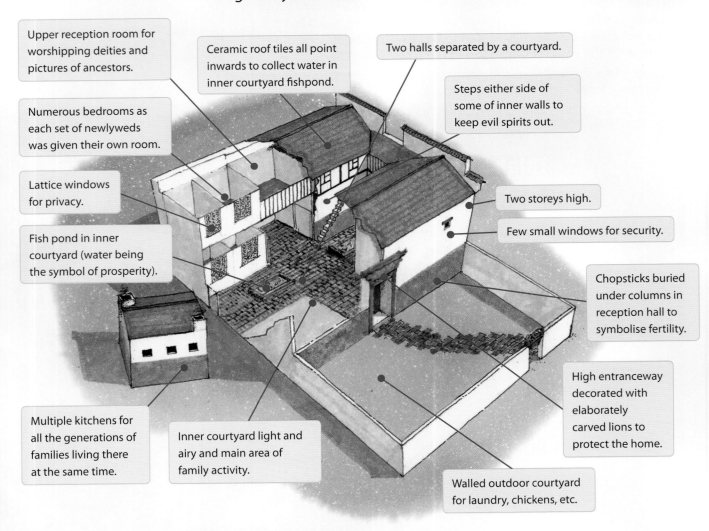

Upper reception room for worshipping deities and pictures of ancestors.

Ceramic roof tiles all point inwards to collect water in inner courtyard fishpond.

Two halls separated by a courtyard.

Steps either side of some of inner walls to keep evil spirits out.

Numerous bedrooms as each set of newlyweds was given their own room.

Lattice windows for privacy.

Two storeys high.

Few small windows for security.

Fish pond in inner courtyard (water being the symbol of prosperity).

Chopsticks buried under columns in reception hall to symbolise fertility.

Multiple kitchens for all the generations of families living there at the same time.

Inner courtyard light and airy and main area of family activity.

High entranceway decorated with elaborately carved lions to protect the home.

Walled outdoor courtyard for laundry, chickens, etc.

■ *A diagram of Yin Yu Tang.*

Your turn ...

1 Imagine you are the estate agent who visited the Huang family when they said they wanted to put their ancestral family home up for sale in 1996. Create a leaflet advertising the house to potential buyers. Describe as many of the features as possible.

Now try this

2 Moving the house was a big job! Why do you think it was not repaired in China and a museum opened there? Discuss this with partner or in a small group.

Think about:

● disavantages of being located in China

● the advantages of being located in the USA.

It is for all these buildings, of all times and styles, that we plead and call upon those who have to deal with them, to stave off decay by daily care, to prop a perilous wall or mend a leaky roof to treat our ancient buildings as monuments of a bygone art, created by bygone manners, that modern art cannot meddle with without destroying. If we do this we will escape our past trapping us. Only if we look after our old buildings can we hand them down to educate and inspire those that come after us.

■ *Adapted from the first manifesto of the Society for the Protection of Ancient Buildings, written by William Morris in 1877.*

In conclusion ...

3 Read **source b**, then answer these questions.

a) Why does William Morris say it so important that we preserve historical buildings?

b) What can we really learn about buildings from their preservation?

c) What can we learn about society, their beliefs and practices from the preservation of buildings?

The life of a Qing Dynasty woman

In this lesson you will:

■ investigate attitudes towards women that defined their role during the Qing Dynasty in China

■ develop empathy of cultural and ethnic diversity within and across societies.

? *Look at source a. This is an x-ray of someone's feet. What can you see?*

During the Qing Dynasty women in China were expected to bind their feet.

Read the following two sources.

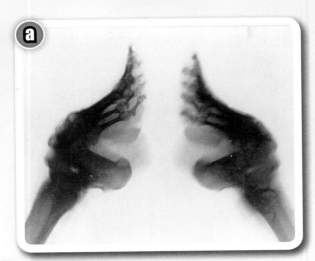

a

b

At last I am free. I was a faithful wife to the man my father selected for me to marry at age 11. I did not complain at his terrible behaviour but fulfilled my duties as a wife to please my husband and bear children. Obviously it is impossible for a woman to divorce her husband unless he has been away for three years – even if he is terrible to her. I had to obey my husband as I had done my father before I was married. Now my husband has died I must live as a faithful widow and never remarry. If I did not have children I would be expected to take my own life.

■ *Diary extract of a Qing woman.*

c

Begin the process at age 6. Cut the toe nails. Wash the feet in herbs, allum or warm animal blood to make the bones and skin soft. Break the four smaller toes and push them under the foot. Pull the whole foot towards the heel forcing the foot to break. Bind in this position. Replace the bandages frequently. Every two weeks force the foot into a shoe one-tenth of an inch smaller each time. The desired length is 3 inches – the lotus foot.

■ *Instructions on how a Chinese mother should bind her daughter's feet.*

How would it feel?

1 What do **sources a, b** and **c** tell us about life for women in China during the Qing Dynasty? Make a list of five points. You might want to mention some of the following:

- choice of husband
- divorce
- the role of a widow
- the role of a wife
- the role of a mother
- how a woman should look.

The Qing Dynasty began in 1644 when invading forces from Manchu took over China. The Manchus did not agree with foot binding and forbade it. However, by 1668 the Manchus had to get rid of this law because Chinese women were choosing to ignore it and go ahead with this incredibly painful tradition. Only Manchu women chose to stop the tradition.

2 Complete the thoughts of the Chinese woman below explaining why she has chosen to go ahead with foot binding.

Opposition to invading forces

Status in society

Obedience as a wife

Potential as a wife

Fashion

Corset wearing

Chinese foot binding during the Qing Dynasty may seem barbaric. However, it bears a striking resemblance to European corset wearing, which was happening at the same time. Wearing a corset left a woman's body deformed. She would be unable to sit or stand without a corset. She would find it impossible to draw deep breath, as the corset crushed the lower chest and forced the ribs to touch each other while moving the kidney and forcing the bowels to sag.

■ *A drawing showing the damage that wearing a corset can do.*

Linking it together

3 Think about the Chinese fashion of foot binding and the European fashion of corset wearing. Copy and complete this table to show what similarities in attitude these different fashions illustrate?

	Chinese foot binding	European corset wearing
Attitude of men towards women		
Attitude of women towards themselves		

Next Lesson

Why did the American Indians move west?

In this lesson you will:

- learn about the diverse origins of the Seminole Indians of Florida

- use sources to investigate the culture, and ethnic diversity of the Seminole peoples.

Who were the Seminole?

When white Europeans settled on the east coast of America in the 1700's the native tribes that lived there had to move. The tribes found new lands in the south-east of America, but even there life would not be settled.

? *What do we know about American Indians and their way of life? List words and phrases that describe what you think are true descriptions of a typical American Indian. Share them with a partner, then underline all the words and phrases that are similar.*

a

■ *An 1830's image of Seminole Chieftan, Thlocklo Tustenuggee (Tiger Tail).*

What was your description of a typical American Indian? It probably did not include fixed houses, fields of crops or black Indians. However, this is how the Seminole Indians lived as part of a settled community of tribes in what is now Florida.

Where the Seminole came from

Unlike many of the American Indian tribes, the Seminole tribe did not exist in Florida before the middle of the eighteenth century. Before this time, the land was part of the Spanish Empire and as the Spanish soldiers spread out across the land, they came into contact with the original inhabitants. At first the Europeans were welcomed, but over time the Spanish sought to control the native populations. However, it was not the soldiers that defeated the native Indians, but something far more deadly.

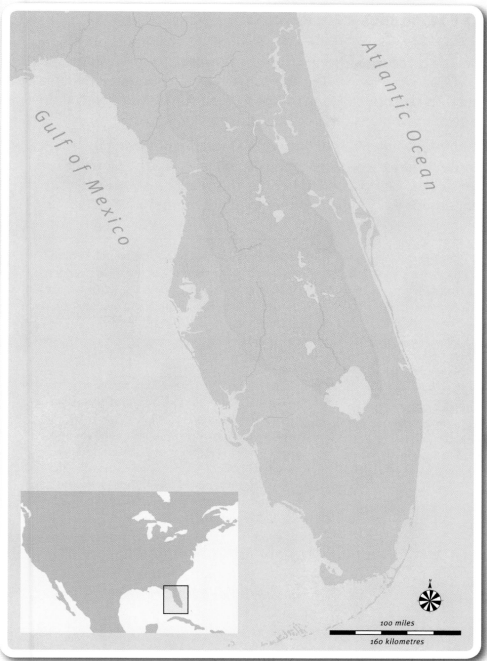

■ This map shows areas of Seminole dominance in south-east America.

b

By the early 1700s, many of the tribes in Florida, including the Apalachees and others, had been destroyed by the Spanish soldiers, either in battles or by diseases such as smallpox. Out of an estimated 100,000 native Americans that occupied Florida during the 1500s, fewer than 50 survived.

■ Adapted from an essay by Dru J Murray entitled 'The Unconquered Seminoles'.

Read and think

1 Look at **source b**. Why did the peoples who lived in Florida before the 1760s disappear, and to what extent were the Seminole Indians responsible?

? *What would make people move away from a place they have lived in for many years?*

Why the Seminoles were different

During the seventeenth century, as the original inhabitants of Florida disappeared other tribes from across the region of south-eastern America began to move in. The Spanish, who had conquered the area in the sixteenth century, called them the 'Cimmarron' or 'wild men'. In the language of the Indians this became 'simano-li'or Seminole.

The Seminoles were different from other Indian tribes living in America at the time. Where the Indians of the Great Plains like the Sioux tribe had a long history of being a united people, the Seminoles were made up of different groups who came together for different reasons.

c
As a result of the Yamasee war, the Yamasee and many of the Indian groups living on the Savannah River fled from Carolina and took up residence among the Lower Creeks or with the Spanish at St Augustine in Florida.

■ *United States Department of the Interior.*

d
The Seminole people are the descendants of the Creek people. The diversity of the tribe is reflected in the fact that its members spoke seven languages: Muscogee, Hitchiti, Koasati, Alabama, Natchez, Yuchi and Shawnee.

■ *Written by Willard Steele, Seminole historian.*

e
The original Seminoles came to Florida because it was controlled by the Spanish. They were mostly Lower Creeks, but other Indians, including Yuchis, Yamasees and Choctaws who had challenged the Spanish conquerors, also joined the tribe during the early 1700s.

■ *Adapted from an essay by Dru J Murray entitled 'The Unconquered Seminoles'.*

f
The British government who controlled eastern America soon learned that Florida was a magnet to African Americans who sought freedom from slavery. Once in Florida, they encountered the Creek and Seminole Native Americans who had established settlements there. Those who chose to make their lives among the Creeks and Seminoles were welcomed into Native American society.

■ *From a website on African Heritage*

■ *Written by David Hackett, a Yuchi historian.*

g
The Yuchi, now only a small tribe, were forced to ally themselves with the Creek tribes for survival.

Over to you ...

2 Use **sources c–g** to develop a spider diagram identifying who the Seminole tribe were, and when and why they came to live in Florida. Look for connections between the different groups of peoples. When you find one, add it to your spider diagram and make a note of why you think it is a connection.

3 If you were able to meet a Seminole Indian from this period, how do you think he would explain his tribe's history to you?

Five Civilised Tribes

The Seminole, along with the Choctaw, Chickasaw, Creek and Cherokee, became known as 'The Five Civilised Tribes' as they took on many of the European settlers' ways. Originally they had been hunters, like most Indian tribes, but the Seminole soon settled in one area and became known for being good at farming crops such as sugarcane, corn and bananas, as well as raising cattle and horses. Instead of tents, the Seminole lived in fixed huts called **chickees** (see **source h**), and some even became Christian.

Where the Seminole were different was in their attitude towards slavery. European settlers used slaves on their plantations in places like Georgia. Slaves who escaped from captivity found a place of safety with the Seminole. So strong was the bond between the former slaves and the Indians that they became known as Black Seminoles.

■ *A modern reconstruction of a Seminole chickee.*

The Seminole nation was made up of different tribes who settled in Florida after the destruction of the original natives through contact with Europeans. Some of the descendants of the original Seminole Indians still live in Florida today, but are not as well known as some of the other American Indian tribes.

Now try this

4 Using information from this lesson develop a Seminole Factfile which helps people who are not aware of the Seminole to understand their heritage and their contribution to American history.

Before you start, consider who your target audience will be. Briefly explain:

● the way you have chosen to present your information
● how it will be organised (chronologically or by themes)
● how it will be written (in the first or third person – 'I' or 'one')
● why your choices are the most appropriate for your audience.

You can then add to this Factfile as you discover more about the Seminole in other lessons and through your own research.

Black Seminoles

Most of us have seen Hollywood films that involve cowboys and Indians.

Before you read any further, sit back to back with a partner. One of you should describe what you think are the main features of the appearance of a typical American Indian. The other should draw what is described.

? *Now compare your pictures to the Seminole Indians shown in sources a and b. What differences can you find from your description?*

a

■ *A nineteenth-century engraving showing a Black Seminole warrior.*

b

■ *Black Seminole Chieftan Gopher John.*

Who were the Black Seminoles?

At the end of the seventeenth and throughout the eighteenth centuries, part of the Spanish Empire included an area of America called La Florida. To the north lay a growing threat: the **colonies** of the British Empire, supplied as they were with an increasing number of slaves brought from Africa to work in the plantations.

For the Spanish to control La Florida they needed money and soldiers, and Spain had a shortage of both. The native populations of La Florida were used to support the regular soldiers, but when diseases brought over by the Europeans began to kill the Indian populations, the Spanish feared that the British would take their colony. Something had to be done, but what?

c Eight black males and two black females who had run away from the city of Charlestown arrived in the Spanish city of St Augustine asking to be baptised. Later on, the chief sergeant of Charlestown visited the city to claim the runaways, but because they had already become Christians and as a prize for becoming Catholic, set them all free and give them anything they need. I hope them to be an example, together with my generosity, of what others should do.

■ *Details of an order issued by King Charles II of Spain in 1693 that changed how slaves escaping from British colonies would be treated.*

d When the English established the border colony of Georgia in 1733, the Spanish Crown made it known once again that runaways would find freedom in Spanish Florida, in return for becoming Catholic and spending four years supporting the Spanish army.

■ *From a website about African heritage.*

Read and think

1 Read **sources c** and **d**. The Spanish in Florida welcomed the slaves that escaped from the British colonies.

   a) Why did they do this?

   b) What would a slave have to do to remain free in Florida?

Living like American Indians

By 1770, runaway slaves were being attracted by the promise of freedom in La Florida. Here they met the Seminole tribes who had a very different view of the runaway slaves from that of the European settlers.

e Though some of the tribes actually owned African slaves, the Seminoles never did. Indeed, many black Africans escaping from slavery in the Carolinas and Georgia came to Florida and built settlements near the Seminoles. Intermarriages and friendships were common. In fact, they were so closely allied that the blacks became known as the Black Seminoles.

■ *From a website on African heritage, University of South Florida.*

f They seem to be free from want or desires. They have no enemy except fear of the white people spreading into their land. They are contented and undisturbed, they appear as free as the birds of the air. From their looks, and actions they form the most striking picture of happiness in this life.

■ *Adapted from William Bartram's book* Travels, *1774.*

■ *A Black Seminole settlement painted in the 1800s.*

h

We found these negroes in possession of large fields of the finest land, producing large crops of corn, beans, melons, pumpkins and other esculent vegetables. I saw, while riding along the borders of the ponds, fine rice growing; and in the village large corn cribs were filled, while the houses were larger and more comfortable than those of the Indians themselves.

■ *The impressions of US army officer Lieutenant George McCall of a Black Seminole community in 1826.*

i

The blacks built villages on the same model as the Indians, living in chickees – raised, palmetto-plank homes adapted to Florida's climate and land. Blacks elected their own leaders and in general conducted themselves more like military allies than slaves.

■ *From a website on Seminole history, outlining living conditions for the Seminole in the 1840's.*

Over to you ...

2 Imagine you are an escaped slave. Use the sources from this lesson to write a secret message to send back to your family to encourage them to risk trying to escape and join you. Think carefully and put in order all the reasons they should come. However, for the message to be delivered safely it has to be small. So you have a limited amount of writing space.

Troubled times

Although geographically isolated from the newly formed United States, the Seminoles and their black allies were aware of its increasing power. Slaves regularly escaped from the plantations of the southern United States, and increasingly plantation owners called for their government to do something to return their slaves to them.

The slaves that escaped to become part of the Seminole tribe legally belonged to the white slave owners in states such as Carolina (to the north).

In conclusion ...

3 Imagine that while travelling in Florida you overhear a heated conversation between a Black Seminole, a white slave owner and a member of the Spanish army about what rights the Indian has.

a) Use all the sources in this lesson to construct the discussion you overhear.

b) You are asked for your opinion. What would you say to the three men?

Andrew Jackson: hero or villain?

The man pictured on this $20 bill is Andrew Jackson, the seventh president of the United States of America. Many people today see him as one of the great presidents of the USA. The Americans put some of their most famous presidents on their bank notes. These include George Washington on the $1 bill and Abraham Lincoln on the $5 bill.

 What type of person do you think President Jackson must have been to receive the honour of appearing on a $20 bill?

Becoming a hero

What makes someone a hero? There are two sides to every story and, as historians, we need to understand as much as possible about the past before we make a judgement.

Make connections

1 a) Construct a spider diagram that helps you to identify the sort of evidence you would need to know before deciding whether someone can be called a hero or a villain. (For example, you might want to include evidence about a person's personality and background or attitudes to other people.)

b) Compare your diagram with that of someone else in your class and add anything new to your own diagram.

c) If you were asked to remove three answers from your diagram, which would you remove and why?

Name: Andrew Jackson

Born: 1767, in South Carolina.

Important dates:

1780: Joined the American army as a courier during the War of Independence against the British.

1788: Became a lawyer and a land and slave owner.

1797: Became the Senator for Tennessee.

1812: Made commander of the US forces fighting in the Creek War.

1813: Lead a US force to victory against Creek Indians at the Battle of Horseshoe Bend.

1815: Defeated the British forces in the Battle of New Orleans and recognised as a national hero by the **US Congress**.

The Seminole

To many white people living in the south-east of America, the Seminole Indians were a problem. Alabama, Mississippi and Georgia were all slave-owning states, and many slave owners were becoming increasingly angry that the Indian population in Florida would shelter runaway slaves. In addition the Seminoles and former slaves had supported the British in the fight against the United States.

Raids by whites into Indian Territory to recover slaves were met with violence. When soldiers and women were killed in retaliation for an attack on an Indian village, the United States turned to Andrew Jackson.

a

In 1817 it was claimed that the Seminoles were harbouring runaway slaves. In January 1818, Andrew Jackson and 3,000 troops began attacking the Seminoles, killing and burning some of their villages. Shortly afterwards the Spanish sold Florida to the United States and the Seminole lands came under the control of the American government.

The Seminole tribe had disputes with settlers in Florida. Jackson argued that the solution to this problem was to move the Seminoles to Oklahoma.

■ *A modern-day British school history website.*

b

Jackson remained in the regular army after the war. Late in 1817, he received orders to curb the Seminole Indians, who were raiding across the border from Spanish Florida. Liberally interpreting his vague instructions, Jackson then quickly conquered Florida.

■ *A brief history of President Andrew Jackson from University of Virginia.*

c

Negroes who have fled from their masters, citizens of the United States and the Seminole Indians all uniting, have raised the tomahawk and, in the character of savage warfare, have neither regarded sex nor age. Helpless women have been massacred, and the cradle crimsoned with the blood of innocence.

■ *Excerpt from a letter by Andrew Jackson dated 23 May 1818 to the Spanish Governor.*

d

Like their Indian allies, the Black Seminoles had suffered a crushing defeat. Their settlements had been burned and looted. Families were broken up and survivors forced south into Florida's uncharted interior.

■ *A modern commentary on the results of the First Seminole War, 1817–18.*

e Seminole Indians captured by US troops in the early 1800s.

f The incidents of this Seminole Indian hunt, which has been dignified with the name 'war', are of very little consequence. It led to the slaughter of about 60 hostile Indians and Negroes, and no white man was slain in the expedition. Several hundred huts were destroyed, and their miserable and deluded inhabitants driven into exile.

■ *From Samuel Perkins' A history of the United States 1812–1827, published in 1828.*

g The consequences resulting from Jackson's action are an honourable and permanent peace. We shall hear no more of murderers and robberies within our borders by savages prowling along the Spanish and British lines to display in their villages the scalps of our men, women and children.

■ *Adapted from John Overton's The start and end of the Seminole war, written in 1819 giving a justification of the measures of the president and his commanding generals.*

Use the sources

2 As reporter on a local newspaper you have been asked to interview Andrew Jackson about his attacks on the Seminole Indians. First, look at **sources a–e**. Then list the questions you would like to ask him. How do you think he would answer any criticism of his actions?

3 Your editor is pleased with the interview but wants to know how other people feel about the attacks. Use **sources f** and **g** to add to your story.

4 Before publication, the editor tells you that you can only use four of the sources.

   a) Which ones would you choose and why?

   b) How does this affect your article, and will it matter to those that read it?

Settlement

Soon after the Seminole War the United States bought Florida from the Spanish for $5 million. Andrew Jackson became the first governor of the State of Florida in 1821.

In 1823, the Seminole Indians signed a treaty with the United States that meant they had to move to a reservation in the centre of the state. In return the United States promised it would protect the Seminole.

h The US government will take the Florida Indians under its care, and will afford them protection against all persons whatsoever. It promises to distribute among the tribes implements of farming, and stock of cattle and hogs, to the amount of $6,000, and an annual sum of $5,000 a year, for 20 successive years.

■ *Article 3 of the treaty with the Florida tribes of Indians, 1823.*

For five years there was peace, but some slave owners were still irritated by the Seminoles keeping escaped slaves. However, despite signing the 1823 treaty the Seminoles still believed that Florida was their land to do with as they pleased.

In 1828, Andrew Jackson was elected president of the United States and in 1830 he passed a law to move the Seminole to Indian country west of the Mississippi River.

i

Article 1: The Seminole Indians relinquish to the United States, all claim to the lands they at present occupy in the Territory of Florida, and agree to emigrate to the country assigned to the Creeks, west of the Mississippi river.

Article 4: The United States agree to pay the sum of $3,000 a year for fifteen years, commencing after the removal of the whole tribe.

■ *From the Treaty of Payne's Landing on the Ocklewaha River, Florida Territory with the Seminole on 9 May 1832.*

? *In what ways is the treaty in source i similar to the treaty in source h?*

? *For what reasons do you think the treaty in source i was written in this way?*

In order to get the Seminoles to agree to the treaty seven chiefs were sent to visit the new reservation, after which they signed a settlement. However, when they returned the chiefs withdrew the agreement saying they could not speak for all the Seminoles.

In March 1835 Jackson wrote to the Indians saying: 'Should you refuse to move, I have then directed the Commanding Officer to remove you by force.'

In the end, eight of the chiefs agreed to move west but many chose not to. It led to a second war that lasted eight years, cost $40 million and resulted in the death of at least 1,500 soldiers. By the end of the war the Indians had been moved.

j

I feel much alarmed at the prospect of seeing General Jackson as president. He is one of the most unfit men I know of for such a place. He has had very little respect for laws or **constitutions**.

■ *Comment made in 1824 by Thomas Jefferson, President of the USA from 1801–1809.*

In conclusion ...

7 Read **source j**. From what you have learned of Andrew Jackson, why do you think Jefferson would have made such a comment? Do you agree with his assessment of Jackson?

8 Look back to the spider diagram you created for task 1a. Using your ideas on what made someone a hero or a villain plus all the sources in this unit, which would you describe Andrew Jackson as? A hero or a villain? Why?

In this lesson you will:

■ find out what happened to other Indian tribes

■ reach a judgement as to the significance of the 'Trail of Tears'.

What was the 'Trail of Tears'?

The painting entitled 'Trail of Tears' (**source a**) records an infamous incident in the Cherokee Indian tribe's history.

? *What do you think is happening in source a and what sorts of decisions might have led to such a movement of people?*

■ *'Trail of Tears', painted by Robert Lindneux in 1942.*

Along with the Seminole, the Cherokee tribe were one of the 'Five Civilised Tribes' that had tried to work with white settlers and adopted some of their customs. The Cherokees had developed a written language and a farming lifestyle. This was not their only link with the Seminoles, though. By the end of the 1830s both tribes had suffered at the hands of the US government.

Gold in Georgia!

How would you react if someone told you that by simply entering a lottery you could win the right to go and dig gold out of the ground?

This was the chance offered to white settlers in 1830, but for the winners it was not as simple as that.

Large parts of Georgia were occupied by Cherokee Indians who had lived there for hundreds of years. They still claimed to control much of Georgia and the surrounding states. However, the state governments of Alabama, Mississippi and Georgia believed the land was theirs, and that the Indians would have to go.

In 1828 Andrew Jackson became the seventh president of the USA and set out to deal with what he saw as the 'Indian problem' once and for all.

b

- The President can provide land west of the River Mississippi where tribes of Indians may choose to exchange the lands where they now live, and go there.
- The President will aid and assist Indians to move to, and settle in, the country for which they may have exchanged.
- The President will cause such tribe or nation to be protected, at their new home, against all interruption or disturbance from any other person or persons whatever.
- The President is to have care over any tribe or nation in the country to which they may move.

■ *Adapted from the Removal Act 1830, a law to exchange lands with the Indians living in any of the states, and for their removal west of the Mississippi River.*

c

Jackson did not hate Indians as a race. But Jackson did believe that Indian civilisation was lower than that of whites, and that tribes who were pressed by white settlers must be absorbed as individuals or be removed to the west.

■ *Modern commentary by Professor Daniel Feller for the University of Virginia.*

Read and think

1 Read **sources b** and **c**.

 a) Source b is a law that President Jackson brought in to help solve the 'Indian problem'. What was he trying to do for the Indians?

 b) Why did President Jackson want to move the Indians?

2 Given the choice of moving from your lands with the help of the US government or staying and 'fighting' for your land, what decision would you have made? Why?

Key words

Cherokee nation
The collected family of tribes that called themselves 'Cherokee'.

Supreme Court
The most powerful court in the United States of America.

The Cherokees were unhappy about the new law from the start. Chief John Ross complained less then two months after it was passed.

d

We wish to remain on the land of our fathers. We have a perfect and original right to remain without interruption. The treaties with us guarantee our right to stay and secure us against intruders.

■ *Adapted from an appeal of the **Cherokee nation**, dated 17 July 1830.*

The lands that Andrew Jackson had identified for the tribes were in 'Indian country' in what is now the state of Oklahoma. Other tribes in eastern states accepted that they would have to move. They knew that the US army would be too powerful for them; the Cherokees did not. They challenged the law in the **Supreme Court** and won the right to stay.

On hearing the verdict of the Supreme Court, President Jackson is reported to have said: 'Chief Justice John Marshall has made his decision; let him enforce it if he can.' It was clear that the president was not going to let the courts get in his way.

Jackson knew that there were a few Cherokees who wanted to move, and he persuaded twenty of them to sign the treaty that gave up their homeland in exchange for $5 million and land to the west of the Mississippi River.

Again, the majority of Cherokees were unhappy and Chief John Ross complained again, this time directly to the government.

e
By this treaty we are stripped of freedom and the right for legal self-defence. Our property may be taken before our eyes; violence may be committed on our persons; we have neither land nor home, nor resting place that can be called our own.

■ *Letter written by Chief John Ross to the Senate and House of Representatives, Red Clay Council Ground, Cherokee nation, 28 September 1836.*

But Ross's complaint did not work and in May 1838, 7,000 troops arrived to forcibly remove the Cherokees to 'Indian country' in what became known as 'The Trail of Tears'.

f
In a single week some 17,000 Cherokees were rounded up into what was surely a concentration camp. Many sickened and died while they awaited transport to the west. Then they were boxed like animals into railroad cars.

■ *From Robert V. Remini's* Andrew Jackson and his Indian Wars, *written in 2001.*

g
Murder is murder, and somebody must answer. Somebody must explain the 4,000 silent graves that mark the trail of the Cherokees to their exile. Six hundred and forty-five wagons lumbering over the frozen ground with their cargo of suffering humanity still lingers in my memory.

■ *From an account by Private John G. Burnett, Mounted Infantry, Cherokee Indian Removal, 1838–39.*

h
Long time we travel on way to new land. People feel bad when they leave Old Nation. Women cry and make sad wails. Children cry and many men cry but they say nothing and just put heads down and keep on go towards West. Many days pass and people die very much.

■ *From an account by Quatie Ross, wife of Chief John Ross, November 1838.*

i
On the morning of 17 November we encountered a terrific snow storm with freezing temperatures. The trail of the exiles was a trail of death. They had to sleep in the wagons and on the ground without fire. I have known as many as 22 of them to die in one night due to ill treatment, cold and exposure.

■ *From an account by Private John G. Burnett, Mounted Infantry, Cherokee Indian Removal, 1838–39.*

Tell it as it was

3 Imagine you are a Cherokee Indian at this time. Use **sources b–i** to create a diary entry or an extended letter to explain your feelings about what is happening to your people.

A new beginning?

By March 1839, the Cherokees arrived at their new home in Oklahoma. Nearly 4,000 Indians had died on the journey, one-fifth of the whole Cherokee nation.

For many whites, the removal of the Indians to new lands was simply logical. It allowed the settlers to gain lands for their growing population, while giving new lands to the Indians in areas that the settlers had no interest in. They thought that both could be happy.

In 1845 a white journalist, John O'Sullivan, wrote that for the white populations, it was their '**manifest destiny** to spread over the continent for the free development of our yearly multiplying millions'.

Key words

Manifest destiny
The belief that it was the white settlers' right and purpose in life to settle the lands of America.

? *Read the definition of 'manifest destiny' above. What do you think O'Sullivan meant, and how would this affect Indian populations like the Cherokee?*

What is the message?

4 Imagine you are a website designer. The modern Cherokee nation has asked you to develop a site to remember the 'Trail of Tears' and its place in the history of their people. With space limited, you cannot tell the whole story, but you have to be able explain the significance of the event to a worldwide audience. Look back at the work you have covered in this lesson to help you. What would you include on the website and why?

5 In response to your new website, a reader has found an extract (**source j**) which suggests that the 'Trail of Tears' saved the Cherokee nation from destruction. How do you think a Cherokee would reply to the reader?

j

To his dying day Jackson genuinely believed that what he had accomplished rescued Cherokees from destruction. And although that statement sounds monstrous and no one in the modern world wishes to accept or believe it, that is exactly what he did. He saved the Five Civilised Nations from probable extinction.

■ *Adapted from Robert V. Remini's* Andrew Jackson and his Indian Wars, *written in 2001.*

How did British industry change with new technology?

In this lesson you will:

- explore how British industry changed with the invention of new technology

- assess the significance of the invention of the steam engine to the Industrial Revolution.

The significance of the steam engine

? *What do you think is the most important piece of technology we use today and why?*

Tremendous amounts of energy are needed in industry. During the Industrial Revolution the increasing demand for power was met to a great extent by the invention of the steam engine.

a A cotton-spinning establishment offers a remarkable example of how, by the use of very great power, an enormous quantity of the easiest work can be accomplished. Often we may see in a single building a 100 horse-power steam engine, which has the strength of 880 men, set in motion 50,000 spindles. The whole requires the service of just 750 workers. But these machines, with the assistance of that mighty power, can produce as much yarn as formerly could hardly have been spun by 200,000 men. So each man can now produce as much as formerly required 166! In 12 hours the factory producers a thread 62,000 miles in length – that is to say which would encircle the whole earth 2½ times!

- *Adapted from Edward Baines' History of the Cotton Manufacture in Great Britain, published in 1835.*

Read and think

1 Using **source a**, complete an ideas map to show the advantages of the steam engine for the cotton industry when compared to water power. Try to add at least six advantages of steam power to your ideas map.

b

	Number of mills	Steam horse-power	Water horse-power
Northern England	934	27,000	6,000
Scotland	125	3,000	2,500
Midlands	54	400	1,000

- *The number of water- and steam-powered mills in 1835, from a modern history book.*

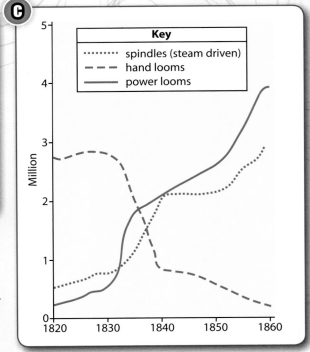

c

- *Graph showing the growth of steam power in the cotton industry from 1820 to 1860.*

2 Look carefully at **source b**. What do you notice about the amount of steam horse-power compared to water horse-power in 1835 particularly in Scotland and the Midlands?

3 Look carefully at **source c**.

a) Describe the growth of hand-powered looms in the cotton industry. Use facts from the graph to back up your description.

b) Now describe the growth of steam-driven spindles and steam-powered looms. Again, make sure you use facts from the graph.

4 Using both these sources, what conclusions can you draw about the speed with which industry actually began to use the steam engine? With this in mind, how significant was the invention of the steam engine to the Industrial Revolution?

The importance of the steam engine

As historians we can debate the speed at which people began to use the steam engine throughout the Industrial Revolution. However, its ultimate significance can never be doubted.

Now try this

5 Imagine 100 years from now you are looking back to today and studying a truly significant invention. Think carefully about the qualities it should have to be considered great. Copy the table below, then list these qualities on the left-hand side. On the right-hand side describe how the steam engine meets any of these qualities.

Qualities an invention must have to be considered really significant	This was like the invention of the steam engine because …

6 Using the qualities you listed in task 5, how significant do you think the invention of the steam engine was to the Industrial Revolution?

Reaction to the new technology

In this lesson you will:

- examine the impact of new technology on employment, wages and the standard of living of 'unskilled' workers

- examine and evaluate the reaction of these workers to the new technology.

? Key words

Benefits
This is money given by the state to help people.

? *Imagine that a new machine is introduced which takes away people's jobs. How do you think these people would react?*

In the nineteenth century hundreds of workers lost their jobs to the new machines that came into the factories. These workers were out of a job immediately even though their families depended on their wages to survive. They had no support, no **benefits**, and little chance of finding another job. Many of them chose to react to their circumstances by rioting.

Between 1790 and 1840 more than 700 riots took place in Britain. Between 1811 and 1816 handloom weavers, wool combers and others resorted to breaking into factories and smashing the new machinery. To protect themselves they made up the name of a leader, Ned Lud. As a result they became known as the Luddites.

■ *This chart shows the impact of the introduction of the power loom on the textile industry and its workers.*

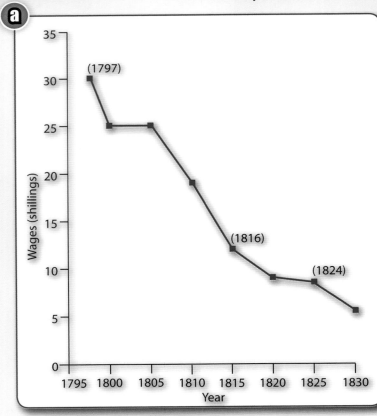

Look and think

1 Look at the information given in **source a**, then answer these questions.

   a) What do you notice about the trend in the number of handloom weavers and the number of power looms from 1813 to 1861? Work out the difference in the number of handloom weavers and the difference in the number of power looms during this period of time.

   b) When did the demand for handloom weavers peak? Explain why you think this happened.

   c) With **source a** in mind, how would the introduction of machinery have been viewed by the following?

   - Factory owners.
   - Unskilled workers.

b

Year	Number of power looms	Number of handloom-weavers
1795	-	75,000
1813	2,400	212,000
1820	14,150	240,000
1829	55,500	225,000
1833	100,000	213,000
1835	109,000	188,000
1845	225,000	60,000
1850	250,000	43,000
1861	400,000	7,000

■ *This table shows the number of power looms and handloom weavers between 1795 and 1861.*

c

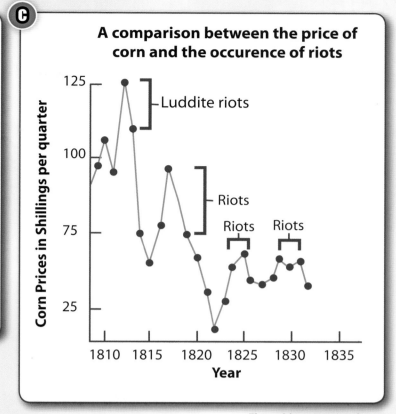

A comparison between the price of corn and the occurence of riots

■ *This table compares the price of corn and the incidence of riots from 1810 up to 1835.*

Who caused the riots?

The government tried to blame the outbreak of riots during this period on people who were trying to overthrow the ruling classes. They suggested these rioters were simply using the impact of the new technology as the excuse they needed to cause unrest.

Compare the sources

2 Take a close look at **sources b** and **c**, then answer these questions.

a) Look at **source b**. For those who were lucky enough to keep their jobs in handloom weaving, what happened to their wages?

b) Look at **source c**. What does it tell you about the price of corn? What effect would this have had on the price of bread?

c) Look again at both sources. What relationship can you see between the dates of the riots, the price of corn and the wages of the handloom weavers?

d) Taking all of this evidence into consideration do you agree that the riots were simply about overthrowing the ruling classes? Explain your answer by referring to all of the evidence.

Argue a case

3 Write a letter under the name of Ned Lud to a local factory owner using all the sources in this lesson. In your letter you must:

● empathise with the handloom weavers

● explain to the factory owner why you are going to wreck his machinery

● justify how you can claim to destroy machines for the sake of the workers, given that by doing so further machine workers will be made redundant and forced to live in the same poverty as the handloom weavers.

How did British industry change with new technology?

In this lesson you will:

- understand the consequences of the Industrial Revolution for women

- suggest a variety of reasons for interpretations of the past.

What was the cost to women?

The effect of the Industrial Revolution on women is a matter of debate. Some say it was an opportunity for women to gain some freedom as they began to earn their own wages. Others argue that women worked because their families were so poor, and their work was at great cost to themselves, their homes and their families. Before you continue this lesson, take a look at **sources a–d**.

(?) *What can you see in this picture?*

- *Extract from a report of the 1842 government commission led by Lord Shaftsbury to investigate conditions in the coal mines and highlight the plight of women workers.*

Betty Harris, age 37: 'I have a belt around my waist and a chain passing between my legs, and I go on my hands and feet. The road is very steep, and we have to hold a rope. The pit is very wet and I have seen the water come up to my thighs. I have drawn till I had the skin off me. The belt and chain is worse when we are in the family way.'

- *These women at the Bryant and May factory were paid 2¼d (less than 1p) for making 144 match boxes and 1d (less than ½p) for making 100 matches per hour. They would be hit or fined by the foreman if they did not work quickly enough and many suffered painful illnesses because of the phosphorous in the matches.*

Your turn ...

1 You have been asked to write a speech to Parliament outlining the terrible **working conditions** for women. Use **sources a–d** to help you. Remember to mention:

- type of job
- pay
- conditions.

Key words

Working conditions

What it is like to work in a particular job. This could include pay, tasks and treatment.

Think about the source

2 **a)** Read **source b**. Why do you think Lord Shaftsbury was highlighting the working conditions of women? Write those reasons onto a table like the one below.

b) Now read **source d**. It too was written by Lord Shaftsbury and makes clear his intentions for highlighting the working conditions of women. Complete the table with these reasons.

Reasons why Lord Shaftsbury highlighted working conditions for women suggested by source b	Reasons why Lord Shaftsbury highlighted working conditions for women suggested by source e.

d When the woman goes out to work everything runs to waste. The house and children are deserted. The wife can do nothing for her husband and family. Dirt, discomfort and ignorance reigns. Females are forming clubs and meet together to drink, sing and smoke. They use the lowest, most brutal and most disgusting language imaginable. A man came into one of these clubrooms with a child in his arms. 'Come, lass,' he said, 'come home for I cannot keep this child quiet and the other I have left crying at home.'

■ *More comments from Lord Shaftsbury made in 1842.*

e The Home Secretary began to explain to the women that a medical officer had reported to him that the heavier hammers would damage their health, especially those of child-bearing age. A very strong-looking woman immediately said: 'I've had fourteen children, sir, and I never was better in my life.'

■ *From Ray Strachey's 'The Cause': A Short History of the Women's Movement in Great Britain, published in 1928.*

In conclusion ...

3 No woman would have found their working conditions ideal. So why do you think the women in **source d** defend their working conditions? Think about what they may be afraid of.

4 Many of the sources used when investigating working conditions are from government enquiries such as the Royal Commission. Evidence is given directly by government officials or by witnesses they have called. Does this make the evidence more or less useful?

2.5d

Taking it further!

The 'Great' Exhibition: did everyone agree?

During Queen Victoria's reign (1837–1901) British trade, industry and the empire all grew. By the middle of the nineteenth century Britain was known as 'the workshop of the world'. Prince Albert, Queen Victoria's husband, had the grand idea to show how proud the Victorians were of their economic domination of the world by displaying together the works of industry of all nations.

On 1 May 1851 the Great Exhibition was opened. A total of 7,381 British exhibitors and 6,556 exhibitors from other countries displayed more than 100,000 products at the Crystal Palace, a building just under 1 kilometre long made entirely of glass and iron.

a

■ *Crystal Palace, designed and constructed for the Great Exhibition of 1851.*

b

■ *British displays contained the most up-to-date machines available at the time.*

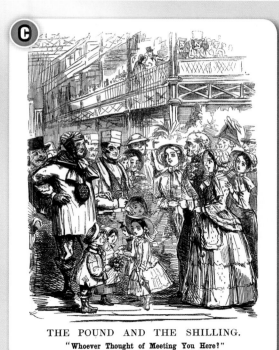

THE POUND AND THE SHILLING.
"Whoever Thought of Meeting You Here!"

■ *This cartoon about the 'Shilling Day' at the Great Exhibition was published in* Punch *in 1851.*

Cheap excursion days, known as 'shilling days', were organised so that middle and poorer **classes** could visit the Great Exhibition. These special days prevented the rich and poor having to meet. Approximately 4.5 million people visited on shilling days.

e

I tell you it is not wealth which our civilisation has created, but riches, with its necessary companion poverty, or in other words slavery. All rich men must have someone to do their dirty work. If competitive commerce creates wealth, then should England surely be the wealthiest country in the world, as I suppose some people think it is, and as it certainly is the richest. But what shabbiness is this rich county driven into?

■ *The comments of socialist William Morris in 1871 about the condition of the worker. He wanted a return to craftsmen rather than machines.*

Key words

Class
People grouped together socially based on wealth and importance (such as the upper class, the middle class and the poorer or working class).

■ *The exhibition included displays from British colonies.*

What can we learn about the Great Exhibition?

1 By the time the Great Exhibition was over, 6 million people (about 17 per cent of the British population) had visited the exhibition and marvelled at the wonders of the world. Using **sources a, b** and **d**, design a leaflet for this exhibition. Working in pairs, one of you should design it from a British point of view and the other for visitors from other countries. You must then compare your ideas and explain any differences.

2 Look at **source c**. What message is the cartoonist trying to give about:

● who was able to visit the Great Exhibition

● the effect of cheap shilling days on mixing the rich (upper class) and the poor (working class).

What are the reactions of both classes to each other?

3 a) Carefully read **source e**. What does William Morris feel is the impact of technology and the growth of industry on:

● the richer classes

● the poorer classes?

b) This source was written twenty years after the Great Exhibition. Is it similar or different from the message of the cartoonist in **source d**? Explain your answer.

Next Lesson

What was it like to be poor in nineteenth-century Britain?

In this lesson you will:

■ investigate conditions in workhouses

■ understand why the workhouses were set up and judge whether their conditions were too harsh on the poor.

● Key words

Paupers
Poor people who received help in the workhouse.

Life in the workhouse

? *What might be done today to help the following people to live comfortably?*

An elderly couple who are too old to work.

An orphaned child.

A widow with two children who does not earn enough to look after her family.

A young man who is injured and who cannot work.

Today there are many different forms of help on offer to these people. In the nineteenth century the only option for them, especially after the introduction of the New Poor Law in 1834 might have been the workhouse.

A typical workhouse

Schoolroom: only a basic education was provided. The lessons were dull and the teachers often beat the children. In 1837 about one-third of all those in workhouses were children.

Separate exercise yards for men, women and children. All except the sick, old and children did unpaid work from 6 a.m until 8 p.m. Work included stone breaking, picking apart old rope, wood chopping, washing and cleaning.

Separate sleeping areas for men, women, boys and girls.

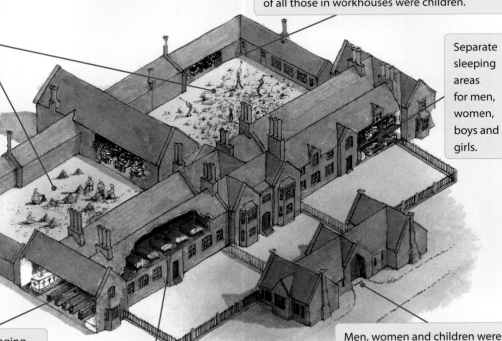

Chapel: encouraging paupers to be religious was very important.

Infirmary: illness was common in the workhouse.

Men, women and children were split up and their possessions were taken away on arrival. They were each given a workhouse uniform.

The food was served up with pieces of black stuff floating around. On examination, we discovered it to be rat and mice manure. I called for the chief officer, who said the porridge was good.

- *Description by George Lansbury, guardian of Poplar workhouse, of the oatmeal porridge served in 1893.*

The inmates had not sufficient clothes and many were without boots to their feet. ' "Poverty's no crime, but here it is treated like crime," they used to say.'

- *A description of workhouse conditions from Will Crooks, a former inmate of Poplar.*

Punishment

Punishment for a first offence in the workhouse was usually a reduced diet, such as bread and water. However, for repeated offences or more serious actions such as damaging workhouse property, **paupers** would be put into solitary confinement for several hours.

9 October: Hannah Hickling spent five hours in solitary confinement for using obscene and profane language and annoying other inmates.

14 November: John Fox and William Crooks had their meat stopped at dinner for fighting.

- *Entries in the punishment book for Southwell workhouse in 1864.*

Why were the workhouses so harsh?

Many people believed that poverty was the fault of the poor who refused to work, were drunk or were criminals. Also if the workhouses were made too comfortable it would encourage laziness and people wouldn't bother working.

However, most people who went to the workhouse were poor because their wages were low or there was not enough work for them all the time, like seasonal farm workers.

Think about it

1 Look at the illustration of a typical workhouse and read **sources a–c**.

a) What do you think a workhouse inmate would describe as the three worst things about life in the workhouse? Why?

b) If workhouses were so bad, why did some people choose to go there?

Write a report

2 Imagine you are an inspector who has visited several workhouses and has been asked to write a report on the conditions and treatment of the paupers.

a) Make a spider diagram of what your report will cover. Think about the following areas: food, work, living conditions, punishments. Remember to include eveidence of what you find.

b) Give your verdict about whether you think the conditions were too harsh.

Give an explanation

3 If the following three individuals had received your report about the workhouse how do you think they would have reacted and why?

- Edwin Chadwick: he believed that poverty was generally the result of idleness, poor education and bad behaviour.
- Charles Dickens: he believed that poverty was not necessarily the fault of the poor, especially in the very young or old; he wrote about the workhouses in his novel *Oliver Twist*.
- A modern charity worker who aims to help the poor and homeless.

What was it like to be poor in nineteenth-century Britain?

In this lesson you will:

■ discover what life was like for poor children in nineteenth-century Britain

■ identify changes to their lives and how far these changes helped them.

Key words

Mudlark
Someone who waded in the muddy banks of the River Thames in search of items they could sell, like bits of coal, rope and discarded tools. The work was dangerous and dirty.

Ragged Schools
Schools set up to teach poor children to read and write for free.

Child poverty

Mr Gamfield smiled as he read the poster on the gate. A boy was offered for sale by the workhouse, and Mr Gamfield knowing what the food was like in the workhouse, knew he would be a nice small boy, just the thing to clean chimneys.

■ *From* Oliver Twist *written by Charles Dickens in 1838. The boy being sold by the workhouse is Oliver Twist, aged nine.*

? *What does source a suggest about how some poor children were treated?*

More than 25 per cent of the population of Britain lived in poverty during the nineteenth century, and life was particularly hard for many poor children. These children usually had no education and it was impossible for them to find well-paid work. Instead, they ended up selling things on the streets, begging, stealing or working as chimney sweeps. Read **sources b–d** to find out more about how some of these children lived.

b
I sell flowers, sir; and so does my younger sister. My father was a tradesman. I never saw him. Mother died seven years ago. I've worked to get myself and sister a bit of bread and pay 2 shillings a week for our room. We can read. I went to a **Ragged School**. The two of us don't make less than 6 pence a day. We live on bread and tea, and sometimes a fresh herring at night. Sometimes we don't eat a bit all day when we're out.

■ *Interview with two orphan flower sellers, aged 11 and 15.*

c
On questioning a **mudlark** who was 9 years old, he said his father had been dead eight years. His mother was alive. 'It's very cold in winter,' he said, 'to stand in the mud without shoes.' He had been three years mud-larking, and thought he should remain a mudlark all his life for there was nothing else he knew how to do. Some days he earned 1 pence, others 4 pence. Some time ago he had gone to a Ragged School but he no longer went there. He could neither read nor write.

■ *Interview with a mudlark.*

d
Q: At what age did you start work?

A: At 6 years of age.

Q: What were your hours of labour?

A: As a child I worked from five in the morning till nine at night.

Q: What is the card-room like?

A: Dusty. You cannot see each other for dust. The machinery was fast and sometimes children got injured by becoming caught up in it.

Q: What work did you do?

A: I was a weigher in the card-room.

Q: Did working in the card-room affect your health?

A: Yes; the dust got up my lungs, and the work was so hard that when I pulled the baskets down, I pulled my bones out of their places.

Q: Are you considerably deformed in your person in consequence of this labour?

A: Yes, I am.

■ *From a report made by the government into working conditions in factories in 1832.*

Your turn ...

1 Read **sources b–d**.

a) What was life like for each child? Make a list for each source noting age, income, parents (if known), education and health.

b) Choose one of the children and identify the main reasons why the work they did was tiring and dangerous.

c) Suggest changes that could have been made to improve the working life of the child you described in task 1b.

Changes to help children

Factory Acts

● No child under 9 years of age should work longer than 48 hours in a factory per week.

● All factories should be cleaned every 14 months.

● Dangerous machinery must be fenced in.

● No person under the age of 18 should be employed in any factory for more than 10 hours in any one day.

● Children between the ages of 9 and 13 should spend 3 hours per day in school.

Other help available

● Ragged Schools were set up by volunteers in town centres after 1844 to provide free education to poor children, so called because of the torn and ragged clothes worn by the children who attended.

● Attendance was made compulsory at primary schools from 1870 for all children and there was no fee.

● Charities and Workhouses provided some shelter and help for poor children.

Spot the changes

2 a) For each child, identify how their lives and work might have altered with the changes above.

b) Whose life do you think would have changed most?

c) Which of the changes do you think would have made most difference to the lives of poor children? Why?

d) How have their lives not improved?

Write a speech

3 Use all the information you have gathered in tasks 1 and 2 to write a speech to be read in Parliament in 1868 by a politician arguing for the need for more action to help children in poverty. You should mention the good things that have been done by the government to help so far but also show what still needs to be done. You could mention:

● work

● education

● homelessness.

Back to the start

In what ways was help for the poor in the nineteenth century different from help provided to poorer people today? Why do you think this might be the case?

next lesson

How did urban life change in the nineteenth century?

In this lesson you will:

- find out why towns grew in size in the nineteenth century, and with what results
- weigh up the advantages and disadvantages of the rapid growth of towns.

Growth of the cities

In Britain today most people live in towns and cities rather than in the countryside. Things were very different in 1801 when nearly four-fifths of the population lived in the countryside. This big change in lifestyle first began in the nineteenth century when there was a massive increase in the size of towns and cities.

Newcastle (87,000)

Sheffield (135,000)

Irish migrants moved to cities in England because of Irish Potato Famine, 1846.

Liverpool (395,000)

Manchester (338,000)

Birmingham (265,000)

KEY
- Coalfield
- Major port
- Major factories
- Migration from rural areas to cities.

Bristol (166,000)

London (3,500,000)

100 miles
160 kilometres

■ A map of Britain in 1851 showing some of the largest cities.

Look and think

1 Use the map and information about Adam Ravens to suggest five reasons why people wanted to move from the countryside to towns.

I moved to Manchester with my family two years ago. I used to be a farm labourer, but I was finding it difficult to get work ever since the invention of mechanical farm machinery. This has meant that fewer workers are needed to run a farm. We heard there was work to be found in the new factories in Manchester, so we came here. My wife and I found work in one of the many cotton mills. I am only paid 12 shillings a week, but it is more than I got as a farm labourer.

Adam Ravens: a factory worker living in Manchester

Living conditions in towns

One of the main problems caused by the movement of so many people so quickly to towns was the lack of cheap housing. As a result many workers and their families found themselves living in overcrowded and unhygienic conditions.

a Families were attracted to the town from all parts for the benefit of employment, and were forced temporarily to resort to crowd together into the houses which already existed: often two families into one house; others into cellars.

■ *Extract from Edwin Chadwick's* Report on the Sanitary Condition of the Labouring Population of Great Britain, *1842.*

b Whole courts and alleys usually have only one **water closet**. Bugs and fleas and other vermin are numerous, so that when visiting such places at night I have sometimes seen numbers of bugs crawling over my clothes and hat.

■ *A description of a slum by a missionary from the London City Mission in 1835.*

c

Place	Gentry (wealthy)	Trade (moderate income)	Labourer (poor)
Liverpool (large city)	35	22	15
Wiltshire (rural)	50	48	33
Rutland (rural)	52	41	38
Manchester (large city)	38	20	17

■ *A comparison of the average life expectancy in different parts of the country in 1842, taken from Edwin Chadwick's Report on the Sanitary Condition of the Labouring Population of Great Britain.*

d

There are thousands of neglected children loitering about the city of London and prowling about the streets, begging and stealing for their daily bread.

■ *Written by journalist Henry Mayhew in 1862.*

Crime

During this period, certain types of theft became more common. Children would sometimes operate in gangs to pick the pockets of the rich. Shoplifters were usually women, because they hid stolen items inside the pleats of their huge dresses.

The growth of the suburbs

As more people crowded into town centres, wealthier people no longer wanted to live there. Instead they built larger houses in the less crowded, cleaner areas on the outskirts of cities, which became known as the suburbs. As a result, rich and poor people living in towns mixed together less as they increasingly lived apart from each other.

Link it together

2 Copy and complete this spider diagram.

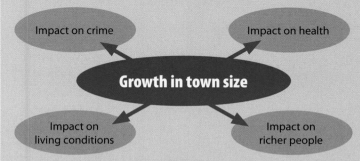

a) Write information on it to show the consequences of the growth of towns.

b) Label each of the entries you have made on your diagram with a + or a – to identify whether it was a good or a bad consequence of the growth of towns.

Tell the story

3 Imagine you are Adam Ravens or his wife. Use the information you have collected in this lesson to write a letter telling your friends in the countryside about your experience of life in the city. Would you recommend that others move to the city? Why? Why not? Try to mention what the city is like for:

● work ● health ● living conditions.

Back to the start

Do you think the advantages and disadvantages of life in towns and cities are the same today as they were in the nineteenth century?

In this lesson you will:

■ find out what public healthcare was like in nineteenth-century Darlington

■ identify ways in which Local Boards of Health improved conditions in towns.

Public health

Disease was common in Victorian towns, not least because of the unhygienic conditions. To help stop the spread of disease, the government encouraged Local Boards of Health to be set up. Their job was to make improvements to clean up towns and cities. They were paid for by extra local taxes.

The town of Darlington, a growing industrial town with woollen mills, a railway and a large cattle market, was one of the first to set up a Board of Health in 1849. The Board immediately wrote a report identifying the problems with health in the town.

? *Look at source a below. What things can you see that would encourage the spread of disease?*

a

Houses in the poorer part of town were overcrowded. Ventilation was bad, as often none of the windows opened.

Most poorer houses did not have running water. People got water from pumps or wells.

Many people kept pigs in their yards or gardens.

Few houses had proper drainage and sewers. Where there were sewers they did not work properly and some leaked. There was no one to inspect and fix the sewers. All the waste carried by the sewers was dumped, untreated, into the River Skerne, which also provided some of the towns drinking water supply.

There was no system for collecting rubbish except that once a fortnight one man, a boy and a horse were employed to clear the streets after market day.

There were only a few outside toilets (called privies or water closets) in the poorer areas. In some yards more than 60 people had to use one toilet.

Houses were arranged around square yards, where pools of stagnant water gathered.

Look and think

1 Look at the drawing of cramped Victorian housing. Select information from it to complete a table like the one below to show the health problems that existed in Darlington.

Issue	Problems in 1849	Action taken to improve health
Housing		
Water		
Waste		

2 Imagine you are a member of the Board of Health. What five measures would you recommend it introduces to help solve the problems you listed in task 1?

3 Now read **source b** to find out the measures the Board did introduce. How many of these recommendations match your suggestions in task 2?

- All public pumps must be repaired and painted for cleanliness.
- All existing privies must be fitted with proper doors and coverings.
- The River Skerne is to be cleaned.
- A complete system of sewers and drains is to be built. Existing sewers are to be repaired.
- A public park is to be created to provide fresh air in the town centre.
- A more regular system of rubbish collection must be provided.
- The Darlington Water Company (now owned by the Health Board) will provide cheaper running water to most houses.

■ *Recommendations of the Darlington Health Board achieved by 1855.*

Problems

Often, the Health Boards did not have enough money or power to pay for all the necessary changes. Many slum areas remained because local people did not want to pay the extra taxes.

There is nothing a man so hates than being cleansed against his will, or having his floors swept, his walls whitewashed, his pet dung heaps cleared away, or his thatch forced to give way to slate.

■ *Written by the editor of The Times in July 1854.*

The principle cause of nuisances in towns is a neglect of duty on the part of the owners of property by not constructing proper conveniences. And is the general public to be taxed because these individuals fail to perform their duty?

■ *Extract from a letter complaining about the Public Health Act in 1851.*

Now try this

4 Read **sources c** and **d**. List the main reasons why people complained about the work of the Health Board.

Speaking out

5 You have been asked by the Board of Health to speak at a meeting in the town to promote their work. Use the information you have gathered in this lesson to write your speech. Remember to:

- tell people what improvements the Health Board have made
- outline what you think still could be done to improve the situation
- argue against the opinions of people who oppose your changes.

6 Now read your speech to a partner and listen to their speech. Write down one thing they have done well and one thing they can do to improve their speech.

In this lesson you will:

- find out what Victorian London was like

- identify ways in which transport and entertainment changed during the nineteenth century.

Life in nineteenth-century London

The London of the nineteenth century was a noisy, busy place. The streets were crowded with people buying and selling goods. As the city grew, so entertainment and leisure flourished.

? *Look at the drawing. What impression does it give of London? Does anything surprise you? In the nineteenth century, London was a strange mix of modern and old fashioned. How is this shown in this drawing?*

- *'A traffic jam at Ludgate Hill, London' drawn by Gustav Doré in 1872.*

Getting around London

Use the railway: opened in 1838, it makes getting into the centre of London quick and easy.

Getting around London

Go by bicycle: invented in 1888, this has rapidly become very popular.

Getting around London

Hansom horse-drawn cabs: available since 1834 and ideal for the wealthy traveller who requires private travel.

Getting around London

Underground railway, opened in 1863: beat London's chaotic roads with the first system of its kind. Trains run every 2 minutes at the reasonable price of 3d a ticket.

Getting around London

Steam ships, operating since 1816: provide regular services along the Thames and to the seaside resorts of Ramsgate and Margate.

Getting around London

6 pence a ticket, horse-drawn omnibuses: makes travel more affordable since 1829.

Entertainment in the city

Cremorne Pleasure Gardens, opened 1846: gas lighting means it is now open late into the evening, offering a theatre, dancing and other activities.

Entertainment in the city

The Oval: home of the first football cup final in 1872.

Entertainment in the city

James Wylde's 'Great Globe', Leicester Square, **opened 1851:** educational and entertaining! Walk into this giant globe for a close-up view of the world.

Entertainment in the city

Stroll along the Thames Embankment: since 1878, it has been lit by new electric lights.

Entertainment in the city

Regent's Park Zoo, opened 1843: visit the world's first reptile house and the largest collection of animals in the world including giraffes, rhinos and an orang-utan.

Entertainment in the city

Madame Tussaud's waxwork collection, opened 1835: for an extra 6d, enter the Chamber of Horrors which includes wax heads of the decapitated King Louis XVI of France and his wife Marie-Antoinette.

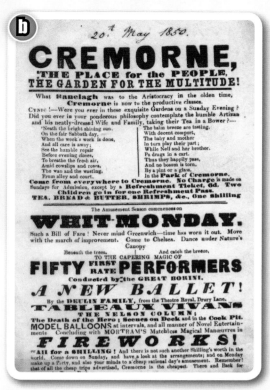

■ *A poster advertising the Cremorne Pleasure Gardens in May 1850.*

Your turn ...

1. Use a timeline like the one below to help you chart the changes in London during the nineteenth century.

1800 1810 1820 1830 1840 1850 1860 1870 1880 1890 1900

   a) First, identify the changes that took place in transport.

   b) Now, using a different colour, identify the changes that took place in entertainment.

2. Which do you think are the most significant changes to transport and entertainment that you have identified? Give your reasons.

Now try this

3. **a)** Use the information in this lesson to plan a day out in London for a Victorian family in 1890.

   b) Now write a postcard or letter from the family to a friend who last visited London in 1830. Explain:
   - what the family did
   - how they travelled around
   - how much London has changed since 1830
   - whether or not the family liked these changes.

Make wider links

4. There were many changes to transport and entertainment in nineteenth-century London. Which types of transport and entertainment from that century would we regard as old fashioned and which are similar to transport and entertainment in London today?

2.7d

Sun, sea and sand: getting out of the towns

Source a is an advert for a railway company offering excursions to Blackpool.

■ *A Midland Railway poster from the 1890's advertising trips to Blackpool.*

? *Look at source a. What can you see in the advert that might encourage factory workers to visit the town?*

Throughout the nineteenth century railway companies built new routes to towns which had previously only been accessible by inadequate roads. As these routes developed, the way in which they were used changed. In 1841, Thomas Cook (a Leicestershire Baptist) had the idea of organising a railway excursion from Leicester to Loughborough. The age of using the train for leisure trips had begun.

For workers employed in factories in the early part of the nineteenth century it would not have been unusual to work from 6.00 a.m. to 5.30 p.m. six days a week. Shop workers could work even longer hours. In 1850 the law was changed to allow workers the opportunity to work a half day on Saturday and have the whole of Sunday off. Then, in 1871, the government introduced four bank holidays, which further extended the amount of time workers had for leisure.

The combination of free time and cheap rail transport encouraged workers from large areas of the industrial north to go to the coast for the first time. Blackpool was their destination of choice. It became famous for its piers, street trams, electric illuminations and its Tower, built in 1894.

Did you know?

The shop WHSmith was set up in 1848 as the official book shop on railway stations so that rail passengers could buy books and newspapers for their journey.

b

■ Bathing machines in the 1880's, which allowed people to access the sea more privately.

d

■ Extract from a poem by Samuel Laycock about workers visiting Blackpool at the end of the nineteenth century.

Why the people go in millions?
Ask the pale-faced factory workers
Ask the toilers in the coal-mines;
These will tell you – gladly tell you –
How the breezes from the ocean
Seem to put new life within them:
How the lame throw down their crutches,
Pallid cheeks turn plump and rosy,
When old Neptune blows upon them.

c

The beach, the beach – the golden sand; the waves, the donkeys, Punch and Judy, sunshine, candyfloss, toffee-apples, ice cream! What more could anyone wish for, except that it should go on forever and not just for one week.

■ A nineteenth-century description at a seaside visit.

What if ... ?

1 What if you were a factory worker going with your daughter and grandchild to the seaside by train for the first time. Use **sources b–d** to create a 'talking head' like the one below either for the grandparent, the daughter or the grandchild. On your talking head, explain:

- what feelings they may have had about making such a journey
- what they knew and understood about the way their world had changed
- what things would have surprised them by their visit.

Before you begin think carefully and make a list of the factors that might influence the way that person thought.

2 Why might the different people have seen the visit to Blackpool in different ways? To what extent should we value their opinions in understanding the importance of changes brought about by the railway?

3 Look again at the poster of Blackpool. Why would railways have gone to such lengths to produce an elaborate advert for a visit to the town?

Next Lesson

What was law and order like during the eighteenth and nineteenth centuries?

In this lesson you will:

- discover the different ways that crime was dealt with

- explain how law and order changed during the eighteenth and nineteenth centuries.

Key words

Punch and Judy shows

Popular puppet show introduced to England in the seventeenth century. Husband and wife, Punch and Judy, were often joined by other characters such as a policeman and a hangman. The puppets were traditionally operated by just one person.

How did law and order change?

In 2007 a woman was arrested for eating a grape that she had not paid for while shopping in a supermarket. The supermarket argued that she had stolen from the store but the police later released her without pressing charges.

? *Do you think the woman really stole from the supermarket? Should she have been punished by the police for eating a grape?*

Many people were shocked that the police arrested someone for stealing a grape. But in the eighteenth century people who stole food were treated very differently because from time to time, food was very scarce. Punishment for stealing food was very harsh to deter other people from stealing. Law and order in the eighteenth century was not much different from the Middle Ages. But during the 1800s things began to change.

■ *Men in the village stocks from 1805.*

The first modern prison, Millbank, opened in London.

1816

1783

Last public hanging at the hanging tree in Hyde Park, Tyburn.

Population starts to grow, along with the number of crimes being committed.

1750 onwards

1717

British convicts sent to Australia for the first time.

■ *An eighteenth-century engraving of an execution at Tyburn.*

■ *A convict chain gang in eighteenth-century Australia.*

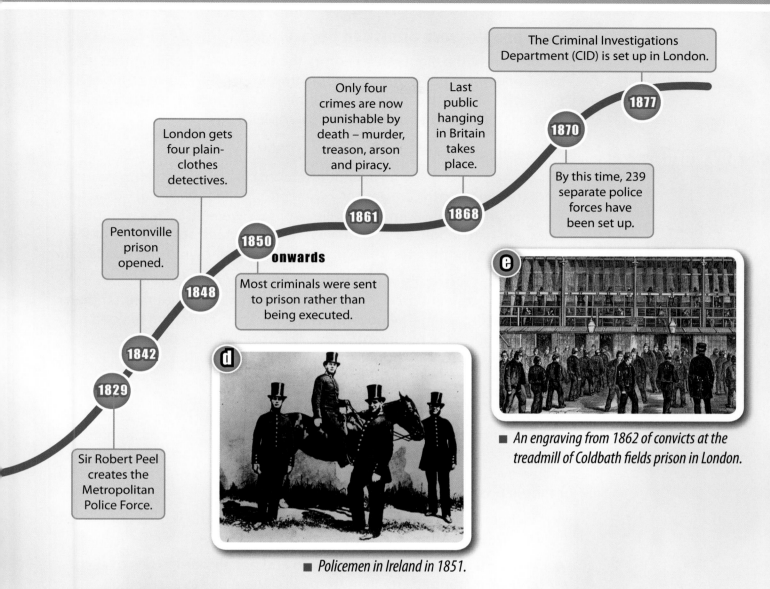

The Criminal Investigations Department (CID) is set up in London.

1877

1870

Only four crimes are now punishable by death – murder, treason, arson and piracy.

Last public hanging in Britain takes place.

By this time, 239 separate police forces have been set up.

London gets four plain-clothes detectives.

1861

1868

Pentonville prison opened.

1850 onwards

Most criminals were sent to prison rather than being executed.

1848

1842

1829

Sir Robert Peel creates the Metropolitan Police Force.

e

■ An engraving from 1862 of convicts at the treadmill of Coldbath fields prison in London.

d

■ Policemen in Ireland in 1851.

Public executions

In the eighteenth century more than 222 crimes were punishable by death including stealing anything worth more than 5 shillings (about 25p). Up until 1868, all hangings were carried out in public. At this time, there wasn't much in the way of entertainment for poor people, so they would often travel for miles to watch an execution. It often turned into a festival with travelling fairs and food stalls. Children would be able to enjoy **Punch and Judy** shows while their parents watched the execution. One problem with public executions was that they provided an ideal opportunity for pickpockets and petty thieves to steal from the crowds.

Look carefully

1   Read the timeline above and look at **sources b–e**.

a)   With a partner, order the changes from 1 to 12, with 12 being the most significant and 1 being the least significant. Make sure you can explain your order.

b)   Now join another pair and compare your orders. Are they the same? Explain your ordering to the other pair and listen to their explanation. Do you want to make any changes to you order?

How people were punished before 1860

At the start of the eighteenth century the government realised that public executions were not deterring people from committing crimes. It began to look for alternative forms of punishments such as **transportation** to Australia, fines, flogging and sending people to prison.

Pioneering prisons

Prisons had existed as a form of punishment since the thirteenth century. Until the nineteenth century, they were often called Houses of Correction. Prisoners, many of whom died while in prison, were punished with boring tasks and hard labour such as moving heavy stones from one side of the courtyard to another. They also had to pay for their own clothes and food.

But although prison life was hard, it did not deter people from committing crimes. Prison life made the prisoners very bitter rather than **rehabilitating** them. The government knew that something needed to be done, so during the nineteenth century inspectors began to visit prisons and report back on the poor and dangerous conditions.

Change to the prisons

Inspectors and prison reformers insisted there should be a switch from humiliating prisoners to rehabilitation. They argued that hard labour made prisoners angry, but giving them time to think about their crimes would eventually rehabilitate them. Two new systems were introduced to modern prisons that would help to enable this.

- *Separate system:* prisoners lived in single cells so they could think about the crimes they had committed and not want to commit them again.

- *Silent system:* prisoners were isolated and not allowed to talk to each other. This stopped criminals from passing on tips to each other.

In 1852, transportation to Australia ended and British prisons struggled to cope with the growing number of prisoners. The government made changes to try to help. They reduced the sentences for many crimes and allowed prisoners who behaved well to be released early.

People also began to demand that schools should be set up in prisons because it was believed that a good education would stop people from committing crimes. Reform Schools for young offenders were first established in 1854 where criminals were able to learn skills such as gardening and woodwork which would help them to find work on their release.

However, many prisons in Britain continued to use physical punishment such as whipping, walking on a treadmill or turning the crank handle all day long. But by 1899 the use of the crank handle and treadmill had been abolished and newly opened prisons operated under the new conditions.

Key words

Rehabilitating
Helping a prisoner to understand how they could live honestly after they left prison.

Transportation
Taking those convicted of crimes to a foreign country as a form of punishment.

■ The crank handle punishment required prisoners to turn a handle all day long and was boring and painful. An engraving from 1884.

Over to you ...

2 In pairs, imagine that one of you is a prison inspector and the other is a prison governor at the time of these changes.

- The prison inspector needs to write a short argument in favour of the new prison systems.
- The governor should write an argument against the new prison systems.

3 Now working individually, design the front cover of a newspaper and use your argument as the front page story. Don't forget to include an eye-catching headline.

Did everyone approve of the new system?

Many people opposed these reforms, especially the 'silent system' and the 'separate system'. They claimed that some prisoners who were kept alone for long periods of time went mad.

In conclusion ...

7 Imagine you are a prison inspector in 1858. Your job is to inspect prisons and write a report about the punishments of inmates. In your report make sure you include:

- a summary of changes that have been made to prisons
- what effect these changes have had on the prisoners
- what other changes you think still need to be made and why.

2.8b

What was law and order like during the eighteenth and nineteenth centuries?

In this lesson you will:

■ understand the role of the Metropolitan police from 1829 onwards

■ use sources to find out what people thought of the new police force at the time.

Were Britain's first policemen popular?

? *What do you think makes a good policeman today?*

With the arrival of the railway and the introduction of national newspapers in the early 1800s, petty theft, robbery and murder appeared to be on the increase in London and politicians were worried. In 1829, to help combat crime, the prime minister, Sir Robert Peel, decided to create a Metropolitan Police Force in London. This was the first official police force in Great Britain.

Policemen were given the nickname Bobbies or Peelers after Sir Robert Peel.

There were approximately only 3,000 policemen in London 1829.

They received no police training apart from a few basic military **drills**.

Policemen only earned 95p a week, which was less than a skilled worker at the time.

Many early police **recruits** were drunks and were quickly fired.

They wore a long dark blue coat and tall hat which made them stand out in London.

They carried a truncheon and a whistle to call for help.

■ *Tom Smith, an early member of Peel's police force.*

Key words

Drill
A regular training routine.

Recruits
People who joined the police force.

Your turn ...

1 Look carefully at **source a**.

a) What can you learn about the new Metropolitan Police Force from this picture?

b) What does it tell you about how effective the first policemen might have been?

c) What skills and equipment do you think the new policemen would have needed to be effective?

Which of these do you think would have been most useful in preventing crime in the nineteenth century? Rank your ideas from most important to least important.

e) Compare your list with the person sitting next to you. How are your lists similar or different? Make sure you are able to justify your order.

Finding out more

One way to find out more about the new police force is to look at sources from the 1830s. For example, **source b** shows new police recruits and provides us with clues about what the artist thought of the police.

The London population was so upset with the introduction of the police force that posters were put up around London openly encouraging people to attack the new Bobbies and even suggested insulting nicknames for them.

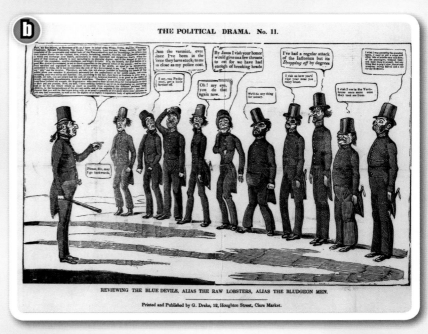

■ *A cartoon published in a newspaper in 1833. The caption reads ' Reviewing the Blue Devils, alias the Raw Lobsters, alias the Bludgeon Men.'*

Over to you ...

2 Look at **source b**. Work with a partner to list the problems it suggests there were with the new policemen. Then answer the questions below.

a) Do you think the source supports the new police force or criticises it?

b) What evidence from the source can you find to back up your point of view?

c) The source is a cartoon printed in a newspaper. With that in mind, do you think this is a realistic image of the police force? Why?

In conclusion ...

3 All sources provide us with historical information but how useful do you think a cartoon (such as **source b**) is for learning about history? Remember, cartoons often exaggerate people's impressions and opinions about things in order to sell newspapers. To help you answer this question ask yourself the 5Ws (see page 182).

4 Apart from the cartoon, what other types of evidence could be used to tell you what policemen in the nineteenth century were like? Once you have compiled a list, explain why each type of evidence would be useful to historians studying the history of crime in Great Britain.

Back to the start

Think back to what you have learned in this enquiry. What do you think was the most important change to law and order in the nineteenth century? Why?

2.8c

Taking it further!

Catching Jack the Ripper!

In 1888 a murderer called Jack the Ripper killed five women in the East End of London. The police printed over 80,000 leaflets asking for help. They also trained bloodhounds for the first time. But they never caught the 'Ripper'. More than 100 years later people are still trying to work out Jack the Ripper's real identity from evidence that was found at the scene of the crimes.

Evidence

Why was it that the Whitechapel Murderer was never caught? Take a look at the primary and secondary evidence in this lesson then complete the task on page 125 about why the police found it so difficult to catch Jack the Ripper.

a

■ *Two different impressions of the possible murderer from the* Illustrated Police News, *20 October 1888.*

b
The police took photographs of the victim's eyes because they believed they would see an image of the last person the victim saw – the Whitechapel Murderer. This was one of the few forensic techniques they could use to investigate crimes.

■ *Taken from a modern textbook.*

c
It was very dark. The man was of average height, may have been left- or right-handed and was wearing a hat. He had his back to me but seemed to be a foreigner. I did not hear him speak and he seemed to disappear into the dark night.

■ *A witness statement from 1888.*

d
■ *This writing was found above the body of Catherine Eddowes, murdered on 30 September 1888 It says: 'The Juwes are not the men that will be blamed for nothing.' The police officer in charge of the case ordered the writing to be scrubbed off the wall. He was afraid that Whitechapel residents would attack Jewish residents.*

Ripper profile
- He was a white male.
- He was average or below average height.
- He was between 20 and 40 years old.
- He did not dress as a labourer or homeless person.
- He lived in the East End of London.
- He could be a doctor.
- He might have been a foreigner.
- He was right-handed.
- He probably had a regular job, as murders took place at the weekend.
- He was probably single so that he could commit the murders.

■ *The police did not have any suspects for the 'Ripper' murders in 1888 but they did come up with a profile of what the murderer could be like.*

Who were the police looking for?

There are two points of view about the identity of the 'Ripper'.

The 'Ripper': View 1

He was educated and upper class. The manner in which he killed people suggested he was a well-trained doctor or a person used to gutting animals such as deer during weekend hunts.

The 'Ripper': View 2

He was uneducated and working class. The fact that he worked in the east of London and used bad spelling and grammar in 'letters' that he may have sent to the newspapers at the time suggests this.

Work it out!

Using the sources and information on these pages, investigate why the police found it so difficult to catch Jack the Ripper.

1 Copy and complete the table below using **sources a–e**. Make sure you think about why you are sorting your evidence in this way. Then highlight any similarities between what the sources are saying.

Source	What it says about the identity of the 'Ripper'	What it says about the problems the police might have had solving the case
a		
b		
c		
d		
e		

2 Use the information from your table to write a report explaining why you think the police could not solve the Whitechapel murders in 1888. Remember to back up your suggestions with information from the sources. You might like to use the following sentences to help you write your report.

In my opinion I feel the main reason why the Whitechapel murderer was never caught was...

I think this because...

Although we can't be certain, source ___ makes me think the police could not catch Jack the Ripper because...

Culture swap

In this unit you have examined the changing lifestyles of some of the people who lived in Britain, America and the Qing Dynasty between 1603 and 1901. Look at the images of the three different cultures below. Then complete the tasks on the next page.

Great Britain

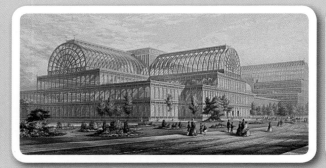

Qing Dynasty

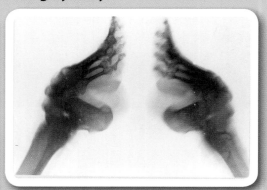

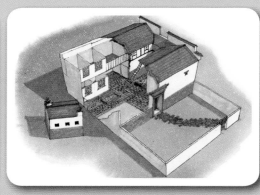

American Indians

Working in pairs, your task is to plan an episode of a new television show in which people from two different historical cultures swap lifestyles for a week. The show needs to explain clearly how these cultures are similar and/or different.

To help you plan your episode you will need to do the following:

- Decide which two cultures you are comparing.

- Select what parts of their lives you will be most interested in filming, e.g. fashion, housing, health etc. Use information from this unit to help you.

- Produce a storyboard for the episode that you will film.

Storyboard: images and captions:

1 You are going to shoot six scenes for each culture you choose. This means that you need to come up with six different images and captions for each culture for your storyboard.

- Select your twelve images to include in your storyboard and plan out how you are going to use these. Make sure that you select aspects in that people will find most interesting.

- The images you select could be ones you have seen in this book, or you might like to find your own images by looking in the library or on the Internet.

- Once you have selected your images write a caption for the bottom of each storyboard picture explaining what you will be showing on film.

Scriptwriting

2 Once you have completed your storyboards in pairs you will each select one of the cultures and write a five-minute script for one of the cultures you have selected.

When you have completed your script, swap with your partner and read each other's work.

As you read through, think of one thing your partner has done well and one suggestion you can make for how they can improve their script.

A little bit extra...

3 Once you have a completed storyboard and script imagine that you are a television critic reviewing the episode that you have produced. Write a short review summarising:

- what the programme is about
- what you have learnt from it.

Keep it short! Your review should be no more than 200 words long. Try reading some magazine and newspaper reviews to gain an idea of writing styles for your television review.

Assessment 1

What were the most important changes in living conditions in Britain between 1603 and 1900?

You have been asked to come up with ideas for a website about the most important changes to living conditions in Britain between 1603 and 1900. Your website will have five sections or pages so you will have to carefully select the five events or inventions that you think made the biggest impact on people's lives.

For each event or invention that you select, write a summary of what you are going to include on that web page. In your summary you will need to explain:

- what change you are covering on that page
- how it changed people's lives
- why you believe it changed Britain dramatically
- what evidence you are going to use to back up your claims.

Each summary should not be more than 100 words long. Remember, you will be writing five summaries in total.

Look back over this unit to remind yourself of some of the changes that took place. You can also use the items below as a starting point.

■ *An engraving of a mudlark from the 1890s.*

■ *An engraving of the cramped living conditions in 1852.*

■ *Blackpool beach and Tower in the 1890s.*

How should you select your five changes?

- Look back over Unit 2 and write down all of the improvements that you feel would be good to include.

- Once you have a list of changes go through it and select the five that you think had the biggest impact upon people in Britain.

- Remember to explain how each change affected people. For example, you could select the invention of trains. You would then describe how trains allowed people who worked in towns to travel to the seaside for holidays and explain why this improved their lives by providing them with quality leisure time.

- Do not just choose inventions but events as well. Remember that people and political movements changed Britain just as much as inventions did.

- Work out what made your change so important and carefully plan out what you are going to say about it.

How to present your summary

- Each summary needs to be short, sharp and snappy.

- You could present each summary as a slide in a PowerPoint® presentation.

How will your work be marked?
Have you:

Level 4
Described five key changes in nineteenth-century Britain?

Said how each change was important?

Explained one way in which each change altered people's lives?

Used dates and historical words correctly?

Level 5
Described five key changes in more detail and put them in the right time frame?

Selected and used information to show why each change was important?

Explained how each change altered people's lives and started to make links between these?

Used the correct historical terms?

Level 6
Described in detail the different types of five changes that were taking place in Britain in the nineteenth century?

Shown what criteria you have used to decide which are the most important changes?

Explained how and why each change altered people's lives and made links between these?

Selected, organised and used relevant information and the correct historical terms?

Were pauper apprentices in nineteenth-century factories all treated the same?

Large factories would often buy children from workhouses and orphanages and set them to work. They were known as pauper apprentices.

Study the sources below and answer the questions that follow them.

a

In the room they entered, the dirty, ragged miserable crew. Lean and distorted limbs – sallow and sunken cheeks – dim hollow eyes... a look of hideous premature old age.

■ *Extract from* Michael Armstrong: Factory Boy, *written by Frances Trollope in 1840. This book described working conditions for pauper apprentices.*

1 Source a comes from a fictional novel written by Frances Trollope in 1840. What can you learn from **source a** about the health of pauper apprentices who worked in factories during the Industrial Revolution?

b

At a little distance from the factory stands a handsome house, two stories high, built for the accommodation of the female apprentices. They are well fed, clothed and educated. The apprentices have milk-porridge for breakfast, potatoes and bacon for dinner, and meat on Sundays.

■ *From* The Philosophy of Manufactures *by Andrew Ure in 1835.*

2 Sources a and **b** give very different impressions of the way that pauper apprentices were treated by factory owners.

   a) Does this mean that one of them is wrong? Explain your answer.

   b) Which source do you think is more reliable? Why?

3 Do you think **source c** supports **source a** or **source b** best? Explain your answer.

c

■ *This picture was painted for the book* Michael Armstrong: Factory Boy *by Trollope, 1840. It shows factory children eating scraps from a pig's trough.*

d

Some pauper apprentices worked in factories owned by caring factory owners. They were well fed, educated and were taught a trade. Other children were unlucky and became cheap slave labour. They were often injured by the dangerous factory machinery.

■ *Taken from a modern history textbook.*

4 Source d was written by a modern historian. Explain: how it agrees and disagrees with the previous sources about how pauper apprentices were treated.

5 Using all four sources and your own knowledge from this unit, answer the question: *Were pauper apprentices in factories all treated the same in the nineteenth century?*

How are you going to complete a task like this?

1 Do not just repeat what is written in **source a**. Think carefully about what the source tells you and what conclusion (inference) you can draw from this. For example, if it describes the condition of the clothes that the children wore, how might this affect their health?

2 This question asks you to compare and contrast (cross reference) two sources. On the surface these are both primary sources and should describe the same conditions, but this is not the case. Think about the following:

● Frances Trollope wrote fictional stories that would be read for pleasure

● Andrew Ure visited factories in the 1830s and wrote about the working conditions that he saw.

Could Frances Trollope have exaggerated the information in her books? Might the two sources describe working conditions in the same factory or in different factories?

3 This question asks you to cross reference again. You must look at not only the picture but the caption that goes with **source c**. When you have made a decision you must explain why you reached the decision in your answer. Make sure you use evidence from the sources.

4 Read through **source d** and look for evidence to suggest that it agrees with the previous sources. Now read it again and look for evidence to suggest that it disagees. Once you have reached your decision explain your answer.

5 Finally you need to use the sources and your own knowledge. Think about the following when answering the question:

● Do the different sources agree or disagree with your own opinions about working conditions in factories?

● Do you think that working conditions were poor for all pauper apprentices?

How will your work be marked?

Have you:

Level 4
Described what life was like for the pauper apprentices, demonstrating that you can interpret information written at the time?

Shown that you understand that people have different points of view about working conditions in the past?

Selected the right information to answer the question appropriately? Written in clear and simple sentences using the correct dates and historical terms?

Level 5
Demonstrated that you understand how factories across Britain might treat pauper apprentices differently?

Been able to suggest more than one reason why people in the past have different points of view about factory conditions?

Selected the correct information to produce a well-structured answer?

Level 6
Shown that you understand how factories across Britain might treat pauper apprentices differently and why people at the time had such different opinions about working conditions?

Been able to suggest more than one reason why people in the past have different points of view about factory conditions and explain why all of these opinions are important?

Selected and organised the correct information to best answer the question?

Unit 3
Moving and travelling

Introduction

It is 1603, and you have travelled the 15 miles to bring your goods to the local market. However, while walking through a run down part of town, you come across a strange machine covered in images and writing. It has the number 1901 flashing in a window. As you touch the machine your world disappears and you find yourself in the year 1901.

Timeline 1603–1901

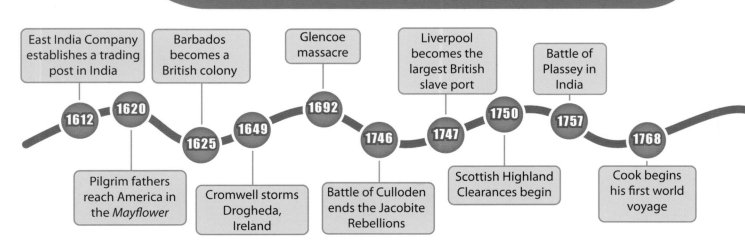

East India Company establishes a trading post in India — **1612**

Pilgrim fathers reach America in the *Mayflower* — **1620**

Barbados becomes a British colony — **1625**

Cromwell storms Drogheda, Ireland — **1649**

Glencoe massacre — **1692**

Battle of Culloden ends the Jacobite Rebellions — **1746**

Liverpool becomes the largest British slave port — **1747**

Scottish Highland Clearances begin — **1750**

Battle of Plassey in India — **1757**

Cook begins his first world voyage — **1768**

As you look around the docks you see all manner of things that you have never seen before. You feel that you must find out all you can, but how?

? **What things can you see that are different from your life in 1603?**

? **What questions do you want to ask the people you meet that could explain the changes you see?**

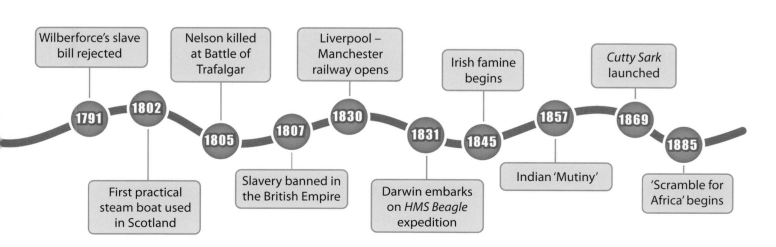

Wilberforce's slave bill rejected — 1791

First practical steam boat used in Scotland — 1802

Nelson killed at Battle of Trafalgar — 1805

Slavery banned in the British Empire — 1807

Liverpool – Manchester railway opens — 1830

Darwin embarks on *HMS Beagle* expedition — 1831

Irish famine begins — 1845

Indian 'Mutiny' — 1857

Cutty Sark launched — 1869

'Scramble for Africa' begins — 1885

What were the reasons Britain wanted an empire?

Key words

Colonies
Territories under control of an Empire.

Empire
A collection of territories governed by one ruler.

a

The silk of India is woven in Coventry and sold wholesale in New York. It is then shipped to New Orleans where it is sold to a planter. That American planter grows cotton that is exported and woven into cloth in Manchester. This cloth is sold in Bengal in India by a trader. The trader may be paid in part in produce (tea, spices). This produce is sold in the English market 10,000 miles away.

■ *Taken from* The Exhibition in 1851 *by William Felkin, 1851.*

Building the Empire

? *Look at this map.*
Using an atlas, list the countries coloured pink.

■ *A map of the world showing in pink the extent of the British Empire in 1750, 1875 and 1899.*

By 1750 Britain held lands in North America, the West Indies and India. These were known as **colonies** and together they made up the British **Empire**. Between 1750 and 1875 the British Empire grew slowly. However, by the end of the nineteenth century, Britain ruled more than 33.5 million square kilometres of territory and about 370 million people of different languages, cultures and religions. Until the 1870s the main reason given for building an Empire was to protect trade. The colonies provided the raw materials needed to make the finished products in Britain. These goods were then sold back to the the colonies.

Make connections

1 Use the information on this page to describe trade in the first half of the nineteenth century. Remember to cover:

● where it travels to and from
● how it is paid for
● what happens to it when it reaches its destination
● who buys it.

b) Using this information explain how the growth of British trade and industry depends on the growth of colonies of the Empire.

From the 1870s the reason for claiming even more colonies and increasing the size of the British Empire changed.

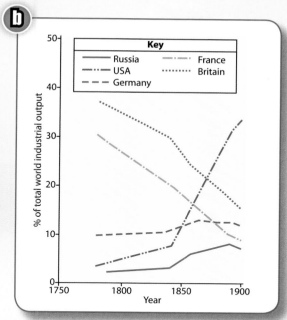

■ *This graph shows Britain's industrial output compared with other countries between 1780 and 1900.*

It is said that our empire is already large enough and does not need extension. We have to remember that it is part of our heritage to take care that the world is shaped by us. It must receive an English-speaking character and not that of other nations. We have to look forward to the future of our race. We should fail in our duty if we do not take our share of the divisions of the world.

■ *From a speech by the Foreign Secretary, and later Prime Minister, Lord Rosebery in 1893.*

Reasoning

2 Using **sources b** and **c** explain four reasons for the growth of the British Empire.

When an Englishman wants a thing he never tells himself he wants it. Instead, he waits until the idea comes into his head that it is his moral and religious duty to conquer those who have the thing he wants. Believing that he is a great champion of freedom he conquers half the world and calls it 'colonisation'. When he wants a market for goods from Manchester he sends a missionary to teach the natives the gospel. The natives kill the missionary. The Englishman then flies to arms in defence of Christianity, fights it, conquers for it and takes the new market as if it were a reward from heaven.

■ *Spoken by a character in a play written by George Bernard Shaw entitled* The Man of Destiny, *published in 1898.*

Explain the links

3 a) Carefully read **source d**. Break it down so that you can create a flow chart showing what motivated the British to build an empire.

b) Where on your flow chart would you put the other motivations of the British to expand their empire?

- They needed a source of raw materials.
- They needed a market for finished goods.
- The desire to be most powerful country in the world.
- Duty to protect natives of the colonies.

c) Discuss your answers with the group. Are your flow charts similar or different? How are they different?

In this lesson you will:

■ examine the human and economic costs of the Atlantic slave trade

■ identify reasons for the Atlantic slave trade.

'A fine business': slavery as a business venture

(?) *What sort of questions would come to your mind if you saw this slogan in a high street shop?*

a

Liverpool	
Cost of fitting out the ship with sales and equipment	£8,018
Cost of goods to trade for slaves:	
Indian textiles	£3,197
Gun powder	£943
Other textiles	£918
Brandy	£620
Arms	£484
Metal goods	£446
Beads	£414
Iron	£357
Medicine	£22
Others (earthenware, wine, etc.)	£1,649
Africa	
Number of slaves received for goods	392
South Carolina	
Approximate value of each slave traded at auction	£70
Money available to buy American rum, sugar and cotton from sale of slaves	?
Britain	
Add 10% for the sale of sugar, rum and cotton to traders in Britain	?
Total profit	£?

■ *Balance sheet for the* Enterprize.

Today, a notice like the one above would be unthinkable. However, for much of the sixteenth and seventeenth centuries the idea of buying and selling people was something many traders thought was absolutely fine. It was considered a business like any other, legal and profitable.

In order to run any business successfully it needs to make a profit. **Source a** gives information about a ship called the *Enterprize*, which sailed out of Liverpool in 1804 bound for West Africa before crossing the Atlantic Ocean to America.

Think about it

1 Look at **source a**.

a) What profit would the Enterprize have made on its trip from Liverpool to South Carolina?

b) How might this profit have been used?

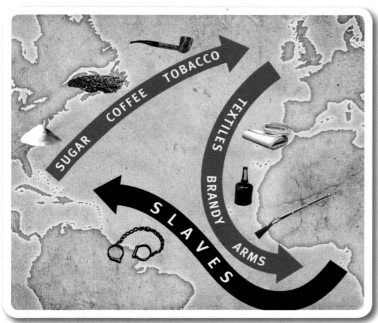

■ *Route of the Atlantic slave trade.*

b

Taken together, the new drugs gave English society an almighty hit. The Empire, it might be said, was built on a huge sugar, caffeine and nicotine rush – a rush nearly everyone could experience.

■ *Extract from historian Niall Ferguson's* Empire: How Britain Made the Modern World, *published in 2004.*

c

Slaves represented a significant amount of capital [money] to their owners. The average price of a prime field hand in Georgia in 1860 was US$1,800.74 Prices in South Carolina in 1859 ranged from US$1,000 for a girl aged 12 to 15, to US$1,500 for a male aged 20 to 26.

■ *Extract from John White and Ralph Willett's* Slavery in the American South, *published in 1970.*

d

Alvaro Caminha established Sao Tomé in 1493. By the mid-1500s, with the help of slave labour, the Portuguese settlers had turned the islands into Africa's foremost exporter of sugar.

■ *Extract from John White and Ralph Willett's* Slavery in the American South, *published in 1970.*

e

Once established on the Caribbean island of Barbados, sugar production increased rapidly, with Barbados experiencing an increase from 7,000 to 12,000 tons produced per year between 1655 and 1700.

■ *Extract from Mark Johnston's essay 'The Sugar Trade in the West Indies and Brazil Between 1492 and 1700'.*

Compare the sources

2 Look carefully at **sources b–e**, which give evidence about why the slave trade prospered, then answer the questions below.

a) In what order of importance would you place these sources to explain why the slave trade was so successful?

b) Compare your order to a partner's. What similarities and differences are there? How would you justify your list?

The Atlantic trade in slaves made cities in Britain like Liverpool and Bristol rich and prosperous. However, by the end of the eighteenth century some people were beginning to challenge this trade, as an inhumane way to make a profit.

In conclusion

3 Imagine you are the captain of the *Enterprize*. Write a letter to those who oppose slavery arguing that the trade is too important to worry about the feelings of slaves.

In this lesson you will:

■ find out about the conditions slaves had to live under

■ use sources to present information to an audience.

Slave conditions

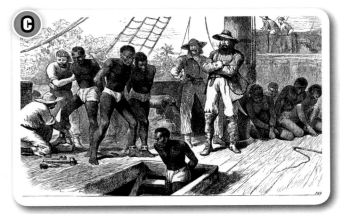

■ *An African dealer marches slaves to the coast to be sold.*

■ *Slaves cutting sugar cane in the West Indies in an engraving from 1858.*

■ *African slaves being loaded into the hold of a slave ship, in a picture from 1880.*

■ *A plantation owner punishes a slave from 1835.*

Sources a–d are representations of black African slaves in the eighteenth and nineteenth centuries. Imagine you are the editor of an anti-slavery newspaper. You have to use just one of these images and create a headline that will catch the eye of a potential reader.

? *Which picture would you choose and why? Explain your decision to a partner.*

? *What would be your headline?*

How do the images in **sources a–d** make you feel? To modern eyes it is difficult to imagine the sort of life a slave might have led, although these pictures do give us some idea.

Use your eyes!

1 Look again at **sources a–d**, which show how slaves were treated from the moment of their capture to the way they lived in their new country. Imagine these pictures are about one family. Select which family member you would like to interview, then make a list of questions to ask him or her.

Most people who lived in Britain in the eighteenth century would not have known about the conditions that slaves had to suffer so that the British could have sugar in their tea or coffee. But just how badly were they treated?

Where did these slaves come from? Some were captured as a result of wars between West African kingdoms like Oyo and Dahomey, where capturing and selling an enemy to slave traders provided a reason to go to war. Tribesmen ventured deep inland to capture others, returning them to the coast to be exchanged for European goods.

At sea

Africans were transported across the Atlantic in slave ships where they were chained below the decks in poor conditions. Not all of those captured survived the journey, but for those who did, life would never be the same again.

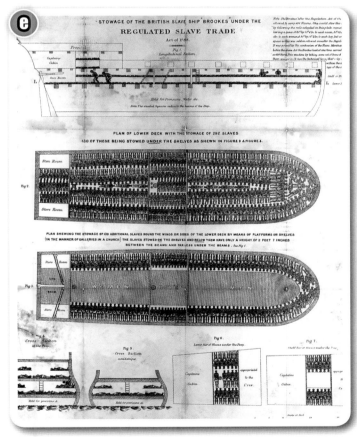

■ *Plan of slaves as they would have been packed aboard a slave ship.*

f
The men, Negroes, on being brought aboard the ship, are immediately fastened together, two and two. However, they are frequently stowed so close as to admit of no other position than lying on their sides.

■ *Extract from Alexander Falconbridge's* An Account of the Slave Trade on the Coast of Africa, *published in 1788.*

g
I was soon put down under the decks, and there I received such a smell as I had never experienced in my life; so that with the stench, and crying together, I became so sick and low that I was not able to eat.

■ *Extract from* The Interesting Narrative of the Life of Olaudah Equiano, or Gustavus Vassa the African, *published in 1789.*

■ *Sailors removing the dead bodies of slaves from below deck, published in 1860.*

i I now wished for death, but soon two of the white men offered me food; and, on refusing to eat, one of them held me fast by the hands, and tied my feet, while the other flogged me severely.

■ *Extract from* The Interesting Narrative of the Life of Olaudah Equiano, or Gustavus Vassa the African, *published in 1789.*

j The hardships suffered by the Negroes during the passage are scarcely to be conceived. They are far more violently affected by seasickness than Europeans. It frequently terminates in death, especially among the women.

■ *Extract from Alexander Falconbridge's* An Account of the Slave Trade on the Coast of Africa, *published in 1788.*

Use your eyes!

2 Working in pairs, study **sources e–j**. One of you should answer question a and the other question b.

a) Look closely at **sources e** and **h** (both visual images). In what ways do the written passages (**sources f, g, i** and **j**) support the impression of what life was like for those being transported as slaves?

b) What in life would have been the most important thing do you think for one of the captured slaves while at sea? Use an example from the sources to back up your answers.

3 Now compare your answers. Are they the same? Did you expect them to be the same? If so, why?

Working as a slave

Having been sold, all slaves could look forward to was a life of hard work. The change in the way they lived was complete. Some were even forced to change their names to those given them by their masters and they were expected to work hard until they died. The alternative was punishment. Children of those brought across the Atlantic were born into slavery and belonged to the master as well.

The sale of slaves

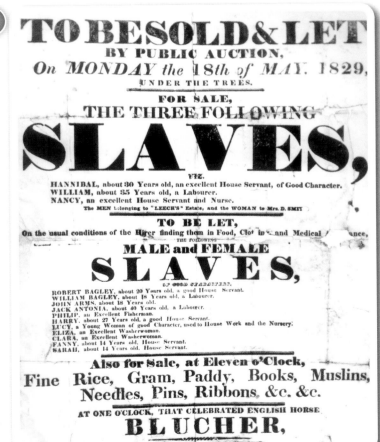

k TO BE SOLD & LET
BY PUBLIC AUCTION,
On MONDAY the 18th of MAY. 1829,
UNDER THE TREES.
FOR SALE,
THE THREE FOLLOWING
SLAVES,
VIZ.
HANNIBAL, about 30 Years old, an excellent House Servant, of Good Character.
WILLIAM, about 35 Years old, a Labourer.
NANCY, an excellent House Servant and Nurse.
The MEN belonging to "LEECH'S" Estate, and the WOMAN to Mrs. D. SMIT
TO BE LET,
On the usual conditions of the Hirer finding them in Food, Clothing and Medical Assistance,
THE FOLLOWING
MALE and FEMALE
SLAVES,
OF GOOD CHARACTERS.
ROBERT BAGLEY, about 20 Years old, a good House Servant.
WILLIAM BAGLEY, about 18 Years old, a Labourer.
JOHN ARMS, about 18 Years old.
JACK ANTONIA, about 40 Years old, a Labourer.
PHILIP, an Excellent Fisherman.
HARRY, about 27 Years old, a good House Servant.
LUCY, a Young Woman of good Character, used to House Work and the Nursery.
ELIZA, an Excellent Washerwoman.
CLARA, an Excellent Washerwoman.
FANNY, about 14 Years old, House Servant.
SARAH, about 14 Years old, House Servant.
Also for Sale, at Eleven o'Clock,
Fine Rice, Gram, Paddy, Books, Muslins,
Needles, Pins, Ribbons, &c. &c.
AT ONE O'CLOCK, THAT CELEBRATED ENGLISH HORSE
BLUCHER,

■ *A slave auction poster from 1829.*

l

We were sold in the usual manner. On a signal given buyers rush at once into the yard where the slaves are held, and make a choice of what they like best. In this manner relations and friends are separated, most of them never to see each other again.

■ *Extract from* The Interesting Narrative of the Life of Olaudah Equiano, or Gustavus Vassa the African, *published in 1789*

m

I was compelled to work under the lash without wages and, often, without clothes enough to hide my nakedness. I have often worked without half enough to eat and laid my wearied limbs down at night to rest upon a dirt floor after having worked hard all the day.

■ *Extract from* Narrative of the life and adventures of Henry Bibb, an American slave, *written by himself and published in 1849.*

n

Slaves' duties could include sowing, hoeing, harvesting, cotton picking and processing, ditch digging, spreading fertilisers, care of livestock, butchering, preserving meats and myriad other tasks. Besides working on production of the plantation's crop, slaves also grew corn and other vegetables to feed themselves and caught fish in traps to add to their family's rations.

■ *Extract from Eugene D Genovese's* Roll, Jordan, Roll: The World the Slaves Made, *published in 1974.*

o

The owner of Roger, a crippled slave, punished him by placing him in an open outhouse, with his back against a partition, and chained to a bolt in the floor and a chain around his neck, the chain passing through the partition behind him. The next morning Roger was found choked to death. The verdict of the jury was that Roger died by choking by a chain placed around his neck by his master – having slipped from the position in which he was placed. No criminal action was brought in this instance.

■ *The case of a slave from South Carolina in 1849. It illustrates that owners could kill slaves in the course of punishing them without being prosecuted.*

Over to you ...

4 Imagine that Roger, the slave who died in **source o**, is your father. Using only the information in **sources m–o**, write a short speech that you could give at his graveside. How would you change what you said if the slave owner was present?

In conclusion ...

5 Choose one the following titles and create a presentation for others in your class explaining what the life of a slave was like.

Title 1: 'Why should we care about what happened 200 years ago during the slave trade?'

Title 2: 'If you were living 200 years ago would you have given up sugar if you had known the truth about slavery?'

When writing your presentation, take care to select information carefully from all the sources in this lesson and conclude it by providing an answer for your audience.

3.2c

In this lesson you will:

- develop a historical opinion using source material
- explain why slavery changed the city of Liverpool.

How did slavery transform Britain?

? *What helps a town grow into a city? List as many things as you can think of that would make your town grow in size. Now look at a partner's list and add anything new to your own list.*

During the eighteenth and nineteenth centuries, port towns like Bristol and Liverpool began to grow very quickly. This changed the way the cities looked and worked, but was it the slave trade that was responsible for a lot of these changes?

Slaves were moved from Africa to be sold in the Americas. The profits from the sale of the slaves bought goods like sugar, rum and tobacco that were sold in Britain for a profit. Much of this profit was spent in the town where the goods were traded, which helped to transform both the town and its people.

■ *Bristol docks in around 1760.*

Towns that grew rich from slavery

Bristol was not the only port town that grew rich on the profits of the Atlantic slave trade. Glasgow and London also benefited, but of all British towns it was Liverpool that gained the most.

By the late seventeenth century, Liverpool had developed links with towns in North America and the Caribbean. Local industries were able to provide the types of goods, like leather and metals, that could easily be traded for slaves. It also had the advantage of a position on the west coast of England, facing in the direction of the returning slave ships. Businessmen recognised that if they improved the docks, Liverpool would soon overtake Bristol as a trading port.

Look carefully

1. Look at **source a**. What can you see in the painting that suggests it might be a wealthy city?

Write a clear account

2. As part of new tourist information scheme at Liverpool docks, you have been asked to write a 100-word piece called 'Changes to Liverpool'. You have found **sources b–f**, but are only allowed to use three of them to help with your piece. So you will have to select the ones that you think are most important and link them together.

b

We are doubling our imports and exports. We have been doubling them since 1749 – about every sixteen years. By 1841 it was 2,425,461 tons.

■ *Recollections of old Liverpool by a 90-year-old in 1863.*

d

The source of much of Liverpool's wealth at that time was the slave trade. The growth of banking was closely connected with this trade. Most of the first bankers were merchants themselves who owned slave ships.

■ *Extract from the Museum of Liverpool website.*

c

	1710	1771
Bristol	20	20
London	24	58
Liverpool	2	107

■ *Number of slave ships registered in English ports in the eighteenth century.*

■ *A painting of Liverpool in 1670.*

■ *A painting of Liverpool in 1813.*

How towns expanded

As Liverpool grew, so the towns and cities that were close to the port also grew. For example, cotton was grown in America and much of it was shipped through Liverpool. From here it was sent to the new factories of nearby Lancashire where it was spun and woven creating thousands of jobs for working-class families there. The wages that these families earned enabled people to enjoy some of the new pleasures in life, like chocolate and sugar.

In conclusion ...

3 The tourist information boards in the docks have been a success and the council now wants an accompanying leaflet that can be given to visitors. They have asked you to write a first person account from the point of view of the 90-year-old in **source b**. It needs to look at how people who lived at the time viewed the changes to Liverpool and what they believed were the reasons behind them.

In this lesson you will:

- learn about what different people valued at the turn of the nineteenth century
- be able to distinguish between the types and nature of arguments being made for and against slavery.

Key words

Fetter
Chains around the ankles or wrists.

Lubbers
Term of abuse for an inexperienced sailor.

Abolition

An American poet wrote **source a** in the early nineteenth century, at a time when there was great debate about whether slavery should be abolished.

? *Who do you think this poem was written for?*

? *In what ways does it make clear to the reader what the poet thought about the slave trade?*

? *What would your reaction be if someone today proudly admitted that they owned slaves?*

If you had asked the final question above in late eighteenth-century Britain, the answer might have been very different from yours. This is because some rich people owned slaves, and the wealth of the cities in which many of them lived had been built on the slave trade.

By the end of the nineteenth century, though, some people were starting to believe that the slave trade was wrong and took actions to stop it. One of these men in Britain was William Wilberforce.

a

'ALL ready?' cried the captain;
'Ay, ay!' the seamen said;
'Heave up the worthless **lubbers**,
The dying and the dead.'
Up from the slave-ship's prison
Fierce, bearded heads were thrust:
'Now let the sharks look to it,
Toss up the dead ones first!'

Corpse after corpse came up,
Death had been busy there;
Where every blow is mercy,
Why should the spoiler spare?
Corpse after corpse they cast
Sullenly from the ship,
Yet bloody with the traces
Of **fetter** link and whip.

■ *Extract from John Greenleaf Whittier's poem 'The slave ships', written in 1832.*

Who was William Wilberforce?

1 Below is some information on William Wilberforce. Organise it into a timeline so that it makes sense. When do you think the turning point for Wilberforce in seeking to end slavery might have been? Why?

■ *William Wilberforce, painted in 1794.*

His Abolition Bill becomes law, 25 March 1807.	30 May 1797, marries Barbara Ann Spooner after a short romance.	1780, Wilberforce becomes Member of Parliament for Hull.	Born 24 August 1759 in Hull.
In 1825, Wilberforce resigns from the House of Commons.	Dies on 29 July 1833.	Wilberforce presents his Abolition Bill before the House of Commons, 1789.	In 1787 he becomes the parliamentary leader of the abolition movement.
He is buried in Westminster Abbey.	Parliament agrees that the abolition of slavery should be gradual, 1792.	Wilberforce retires from politics in 1825.	Becomes a crusading Christian in 1784.

■ *The life and times of William Wilberforce, who tried to end the slave trade in Britain.*

The abolition of the slave trade in the British Empire was not going to happen overnight. Britain had been involved in the trade for more than 100 years before some people began to ask questions about whether it was right to trade in this way. From 1789, William Wilberforce began to argue for the abolition of the trade. He made speeches against slavery and many MPs supported him. However, there were many others, both in Parliament and across the country, who bitterly opposed his ideas.

The anti-Abolitionists

c

The plan for the abolition of the slave trade is, in every view of it, silly and unwise. It is founded on the mistaken idea of kindness, or rather on ignorance, stupidity and passion. The Negroes of Africa, in their native country, are apparently useless in the great scale of human society. They are totally incapable of improvement, arts or sciences. The only way to promote their civilisation, to make them useful in their life, and happy in themselves, is to introduce them to a state of activity and industry.

■ *Adaptation of a letter published in* Gentleman's Magazine, *23 April 1789.*

d

Abolition will bring ruin to Liverpool. Complete abolition would mean financial loss of more than £7 million to Liverpool [more than £6 hundred million at today's prices]. Not only would owners, masters, officers and sailors be affected, but the whole town would suffer as there would be less dock duty, less employment for boat builders, etc., and a decrease in the rents of houses, shops and warehouses in consequence of the unemployment, and likely emigration of seamen, boat builders and men in associated trades.

■ *Statement made by Matthew Gregson, a rich Liverpool businessman who played a big part in building up the city.*

What do the sources tell us?

2 Read **sources c** and **d**, from people who do not want the slave trade to be abolished.

a) Using these sources, create a spider diagram that identifies the arguments against abolition.

b) Compare your diagram with others in your group, and add to your diagram any points you might have missed.

c) With a partner, number the points on your diagram from 1 to 5 (1 being the most powerful) to identify which is the most convincing argument for keeping the slave trade.

d) Compare your answers with another pair and explain your reasons for the way you have numbered your diagram.

e) Take a class vote. Which was the most important reason for keeping slavery? You must ALL agree!

To begin with, Wilberforce and his fellow campaigners were not listened to by Parliament. It took many attempts before Parliament began to listen seriously to the arguments. Eventually Parliament set up an enquiry into the slave trade and began to take evidence from several people so that a decision about ending it could be made.

The Abolitionists

■ *Adapted from William Wilberforce's speech to the House of Commons in 1803.*

e

I believe if the misery of any one of the many hundred Negroes stowed in each ship could be brought before their view, that there is no one among them whose heart would bear it. Let anyone imagine to himself six or seven hundred of these poor souls chained two by two, surrounded with every object that is sickening and disgusting, diseased, and struggling under every kind of misery!

■ *Extracts from William Wilberforce's speech supporting the abolition of the slave trade, 2 April 1792.*

f

Songs and dances were promoted for exercise. It was not a scene of freedom or joy, for one sailor was employed to dance the men, and another to dance the women. If the slaves found themselves not wanting to dance, certain persons were ordered to whip them into compliance.

In every common cargo, it has been observed that about 50 or 60 perish. Slaves are subject to the following disorders: small pox, measles, dysentery, fluxes and fevers.

Slaves were driven in the field, whipped like cattle, and often branded and treated with the greatest cruelty.

■ *Evidence of James Towne, a ship's carpenter who served on slave ships, 1791.*

g

Q: When the Negroes are brought down to the coast, do they appear to come willingly?

A: By no means.

Q: Were the Negroes fettered on board ships which you have known?

A: Always – with legshackles and handcuffs, two and two. Right and left.

Q: Has the space in which they have been confined on board the ship been sufficient for their convenience or health?

A: By no means. They lay in a crowded and cramped state, neither had their length or breadth.

Q: Did you know of any inconvenience arising from the heat of their rooms?

A: I have known them to go down well, and in the morning brought up dead, from the suffocated state they were in below.

Q: Do you recollect the height between decks of the ships in which you sailed?

A: The Peggy was about 4 feet, and the Sally about 4 feet 4 inches or 5 feet 5.

Q: Whereabouts were the number of Negroes taken on board the Peggy?

A: About 230, I believe, altogether.

What do the sources tell us?

3 Read **sources e** and **f**. What arguments do the abolitionists use to support their case? Using a different colour, add these points to the spider diagram you began in task 2.

Did you know?

Denmark was the first European country to ban the import of slaves to its colonies in 1803, four years before Britain.

The USA made the slave trade illegal in 1808, but laws to ban the owning of slaves were not passed until 1865.

Look at both sides

4   People have different ways of looking at things depending on who they are. You are about to decide whether you are in favour of keeping slavery or abolishing it.

a) Look back at the arguments of both the Abolitionists and the anti-Abolitionists.

b) Form groups of six. Then choose two of your group to be in favour of keeping slavery and two people to be against it. The remaining two group members will listen to each of you speak and summarise the views you are making to feed back to the rest of the class.

Those for keeping the trade in slaves	Those against keeping the trade in slaves
A Liverpool sailor	A Christian religious leader
A shipping owner	William Wilberforce

c) For each group construct a short speech to support your viewpoint.
Take care to think about:

● who you are

● why you view the slave trade in a certain way

● which facts you think would best support your case.

5   Using the information from this lesson, develop an extended answer to the question:

'Why did it take so long to abolish the slave trade in the British Empire?'

In your answer include:

● a point of view that you can support throughout your work

● evidence from the sources that outlines both sides of the debate

● a conclusion that explains why the point of view you set out at the start was accurate.

Back to the start

From all the evidence you have gathered from your work in this enquiry, how far do you think that Britain's involvement in the slave trade at the end of the eighteenth-century was simply 'common sense', and how do you think that ordinary people of the day would have viewed it?

3.2e

Taking it further!

How has slavery been interpreted?

? *What do you think the slave trade was like?*

In order to answer the question above, you need some evidence on which to make a judgement (which is exactly how historians work). However, getting at the truth is not as easy as it sounds. Before you decide on which sources to use, each one needs to be considered in terms of its:

- nature (the type of source it is)
- origin (where the information has come from)
- purpose (why the source has been created).

a

Death of Capt. Ferrer, the Captain of the Amistad, July, 1839.

Don Jose Ruiz and Don Pedro Montez, of the Island of Cuba, having purchased fifty-three slaves at Havana, recently imported from Africa, put th...

■ *Image illustrating the revolt of slaves on the slave ship Amistad in 1839.*

b The reason why the Atlantic slave trade lasted so long is that in the Americas the Africans proved to be admirable workers, strong enough to survive the heat and work hard on sugar, coffee or cotton plantations or in the mines, in building fortresses or merely acting as servants; and at the same time, they were good-natured and usually docile.

■ *A modern account of the slave trade.*

Use the Sources

1 Look at either **source a** or **source b**.

What sentence would you write to describe the nature of the source? What sentence would you write to describe its origin? And what sentence would you write to describe the purpose?

2 Review your answers with others in your class that have selected the same source.

How do their answers differ and why do you think they have come to their conclusions?

c It may be asked why I have written this work, when there has been so much already written and published of the same character from other fugitives? My answer is, that in no place have I given orally the detail of my narrative; and some of the most interesting events of my life have never reached the public ear. Moreover, it was at the request of many friends of low-trodden humanity, that I have undertaken to write the following sketch, that light and truth might be spread on the sin and evils of slavery as far as possible.

■ *Extract written in 1847 from* Narrative of the life and adventures of Henry Bibb, an American slave, *written by Bibb and published in 1849.*

d

$150 REWARD

RANAWAY from the subscriber, on the night of the 2d instant, a negro man, who calls himself *Henry May*, about 22 years old, 5 feet 6 or 8 inches high, ordinary color, rather chunky built, bushy head, and has it divided mostly on one side, and keeps it very nicely combed; has been raised in the house, and is a first rate dining-room servant, and was in a tavern in Louisville for 18 months. I expect he is now in Louisville trying to make his escape to a free state, (in all probability to Cincinnati, Ohio.) Perhaps he may try to get employment on a steamboat. He is a good cook, and is handy in any capacity as a house servant. Had on when he left, a dark cassinett coatee, and dark striped cassinett pantaloons, new---he had other clothing. I will give $50 reward if taken in Louisvill; 100 dollars if taken one hundred miles from Louisville in this State, and 150 dollars if taken out of this State, and delivered to me, or secured in any jail so that I can get him again. WILLIAM BURKE.

Bardstown, Ky., September 3d, 1838.

■ *St Louis slave reward poster, 1847.*

Work it out!

3 a) Thinking about nature, origin and purpose, in what ways are **sources c** and **d** different? Which would be more useful to a historian and why?

b) Draw the following mind map:

● in the middle write the words: 'Problems of interpreting the slave trade'.

● on one arm put the words 'Nature of sources' (N).

● on the second arm put the words 'Origin of source' (O).

● on the third arm put the words 'Purpose of source' (P).

Use **sources a–d** to start your mind map by adding smaller sections to each of the arms you have drawn, e.g.:

Source c is:

● **an example of an autobiography (N)**

● **written at the time (first hand) (O)**

● **written to provide a personal view of slavery (P).**

4 Look back over all the lessons in this enquiry. Add as many different examples as you can to each of the arms of your mind map. Compare your finished mind map with others and add any new items to your own version.

5 Imagine you have been invited onto a radio talk show. One of the other guests has a strong opinion that the slave trade was not as bad as it has been made out to be.

a) Using just two of the sources in this lesson, construct a short speech that argues the opposite point of view.

b) Which sources did you choose and why?

c) What weaknesses are there in your opponent's argument because of their choice of sources?

d) In what ways would your speech have been different if you had been able to use more sources?

6 Look at this statement:

'Because there is so much evidence we can never know the truth about the Atlantic Slave Trade.'

To what extent do you think this statement is true and why?

Next Lesson

Assessment 1

What were the arguments for and against slavery?

■ *This picture called 'George Washington as a Farmer at Mout Vernon' was created in 1851 by Junius Brutus Stearns. It gives a sentimentalised view of slaves working at Mount Vernon in the United States.*

1 Look at the image of slavery above.

a) Make a list of the things in this image that you think shows the benefits that slavery brought.

b) Now list those things that you think are negative aspects of slavery.

2 What title might you give this image? Briefly explain why you would call it that.

3 Historians using evidence need to ask themselves questions in order to understand the period that they are writing about. Look at the image again. How useful is it to you when considering the arguments for and against slavery?

4 You are going to use the evidence from this section to create an 'upside down' booklet.

Use three pages of blank A4 paper and fold them in half to create a booklet.

a) On the front page of the booklet write 'Reasons for the slave trade'. On the following pages you need to argue and explain from one side the reasons:

- why slavery existed
- why so many people believed it was a good business.

b) Once you have reached the middle of the booklet, turn it upside down. With the 'spine' of your booklet on the left write 'Reasons against the slave trade'. Use the next pages of the booklet to argue and explain against slavery.

How are you going to set about a task like this?

Question 1

When an artist paints a picture like this one they are trying to give the person who looks at it a message about what they think life was like. As you look at the painting quickly write down words that come to mind. Secondly note down items or parts of the painting that made you think of your original words. You also need to conclude why the artist included these items.

Question 2

By giving a title to an image, you are being asked to identify the key idea of the image – what it is all about. Look at the image and write down in rough the first title you think of. Then take a little more time to come up with two other titles. Compare the three titles. Which is the best one and why?

Question 3

Use the **5xW** rule to help you here (see page 182).

Which of these questions are difficult to answer? Is it important that you know the answers to all of the questions? If so, why?

Question 4

- Make sure that when you are writing your booklet you use sources and diagrams that you have examined in the lessons so far. You will also need to explain any problems that your sources may have. Think about the **5xW** rule for this.

- For both sides of the booklet you need to convince the reader of the argument you are putting forward. Some of the best arguments are ones that are very simply stated.

- To start with think of one reason why the slave trade should be abolished and try to write it down in just one word. Using that word as the centre of an ideas map write down four additional linking words that provide the evidence that would support or prove the very first word you put down. These words could link to pictures, poems or text.

- Build up your evidence by trying to find two more words that can support each of you linking words.

- Now do the same for the opposing idea.

How will your work be marked? Have you:

Level 4
Described some of the features and events of the slave trade and shown that there were changes throughout the period?

Used evidence to show that the slave trade can be interpreted in different ways?

Begun to structure your information to put forward simple arguments for and against slavery?

Level 5
Described some of the features and events of the slave trade to show that these affected different people in different ways?

Begun to suggest reasons why the evidence can provide differing interpretations for the slave trade?

Begun to carefully select your information to make structured arguments for and against slavery?

Level 6
Begun to explain why some of the features and events of the slave trade affected different people in different ways?

Begun to explain how and why the evidence can provide differing interpretations for the slave trade?

Carefully focused your information to produce strong and convincing arguments for and against slavery?

Next Lesson

In this lesson you will:

- **use a map to investigate the voyages made by Captain Cook**

- **explain how important Cook's discoveries were.**

Cook's voyages of discovery

People go on voyages of discovery to find new lands and different peoples, to make more accurate maps and to gather new resources. Over the centuries, Europeans had discovered more of the world, but by the early eighteenth century much of the world remained unexplored.

? *In what ways is the map in source a incorrect? Why might it have been difficult to create an accurate map of the world in the eighteenth century?*

Captain Cook

The British explorer Captain Cook was the first European to discover the east coast of Australia and New Zealand. Cook's voyage on board the ship *Endeavour* lasted two years, and had great significance for Britain and in improving understanding of the world.

a TYPVS ORBIS TERRARVM

- *A map of the world drawn by Abraham Ortelius in 1570.*

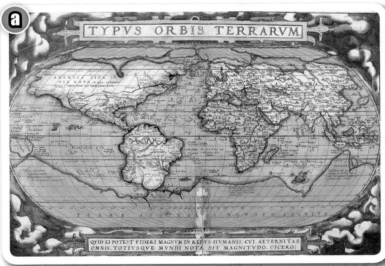

Some Aborigines tried to set fire to cook's ship. Instead of firing on them, Cook followed them into the woods and made peace with their chief. Cook later showed some of the Aborigines around his ship.

Cooktown ●

Great Barrier Reef

A U S T R A L I A

Botany Bay

Cooks ship ran aground on the coral reef here and took 7 weeks to repair.

Cook's crew was attacked with stones and darts by two Aborigines. The crew fired shots to scare them away.

Two scientists from the Endeavour discovered more than 1,400 new types of plant. As a result they named one of the places they moored Botany Bay. Cook's crew were the first Europenas to see a kangaroo, which they found was 'excellent food'.

- *A map of Captain Cook's discoveries in and around New Zealand and Australia.*

Cook also discovered the Hawaiian Islands. It was here that he was stabbed to death on the beach by a group of Hawaiians after an argument.

Cook's voyages were important in discovering new territories for Britain and in demonstrating more accurate mapping techniques. Later in the nineteenth century, voyages of discovery built on these achievements by trying to create even more accurate maps of different parts of the world, but they also often had greater scientific purposes.

Think about it

1 Captain Cook was an important man. Why? Think about what he discovered that would benefit:

● Britain
● science
● people's understanding of the world.

Share your ideas with a partner. Together, list the five discoveries that Cook made.

Now try this

2 There is a big statue of Cook in Whitby, the place from where he sailed. Your job is to unveil the statue and convince people that Cook's voyages where a turning point in how people viewed the world. Make a note of the key points that you will use to do this.

Tell the story

3 Write a newspaper article reporting on the return of Cook from his voyage of exploration.

You should include sections on:

● where he travelled
● what he discovered
● why his discoveries will have long lasting significance.

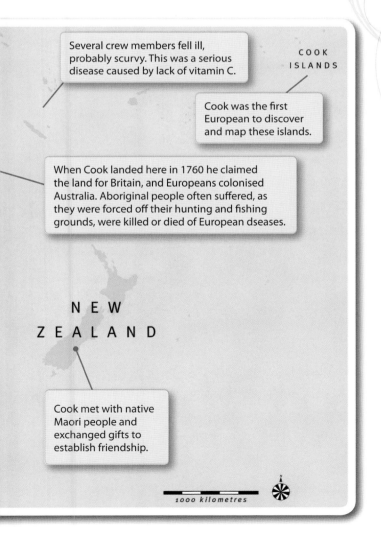

Several crew members fell ill, probably scurvy. This was a serious disease caused by lack of vitamin C.

COOK ISLANDS

Cook was the first European to discover and map these islands.

When Cook landed here in 1760 he claimed the land for Britain, and Europeans colonised Australia. Aboriginal people often suffered, as they were forced off their hunting and fishing grounds, were killed or died of European dseases.

NEW ZEALAND

Cook met with native Maori people and exchanged gifts to establish friendship.

1000 kilometres

An Arctic mystery

In this lesson you will:

- try to work out an Arctic mystery
- use evidence as part of an enquiry.

? *Why do people explore the Arctic today? Why might the reasons have been different in the nineteenth century?*

In 1845, 130 Arctic explorers set sail from London. Their aim was to find a route through the land and ice of the Arctic to the Pacific Ocean. Excited crowds cheered the explorers and their leader, Sir John Franklin, as they set sail in two well-equipped ships, which carried supplies including nearly 8,000 tins of meat, fruit and vegetables.

Despite these preparations, none of the crew returned. There are different opinions about what happened. Some people say they had resorted to cannibalism and died of starvation, others they were poisoned or that they were killed by disease.

Your task is to decide what you think really happened.

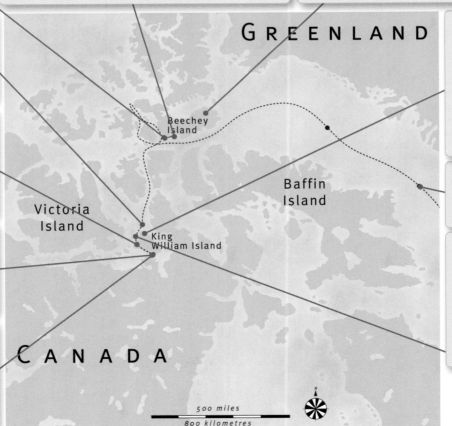

Winter 1845: The explorers set up camp because thick ice prevented the ships from sailing onward.

1984: Food tins were discovered. Some had not been properly sealed, so the food would have gone bad. Also, lead used to seal the tins was found on the inside as well as on the outside. It is likely that the officers would have eaten more of the tinned food than the ordinary crewmen.

1984: Scientists found the graves of three explorers who had died early in the expedition. The men's bodies were very well preserved because of the freezing Arctic conditions. Tests on the bodies showed signs of **tuberculosis**, starvation, **scurvy** and lead poisoning.

September 1846: The explorers abandoned their ice-trapped ships and set off on sledges to find supplies and safety.

Skeletons were found at Terror Bay and Starvation Cove. These are believed to be the explorers who died after leaving their ships.

1981: A skeleton of one of the explorers was found showing tiny cut marks on the bone. These looked like knife marks.

Scientists tested the bones, which showed signs of lead poisoning. This can cause loss of appetite, confusion, irritability and weakness.

1854: John Rae, an explorer, met Eskimos who said that Franklin's men had been suffering from starvation, looked confused and weak and that some of them had resorted to cannibalism.

May 1845: Franklin's expedition entered the waters of the Arctic

1857: A note from the explorers was found. It said that the ships had been trapped in ice, and that nine officers and fifteen crew were dead. It gave no reason for the deaths.

GREENLAND

Beechey Island

Baffin Island

Victoria Island

King William Island

CANADA

500 miles

800 kilometres

■ *A map of Sir John Franklin's Arctic voyage showing some of the things that went wrong.*

The preseved body of John Torrington, one of the expedition whose body was discovered in 1984.

Cannibalism

Charles Dickens, the writer, wrote an article criticising the view that the explorers had resorted to cannibalism (see **source b**).

b

The Eskimo evidence is unreliable for at the very best it was given second hand through an interpreter who, in all probability, did not fully understand the language he translated. I also believe it is improbable that such courageous, strong and religious men as the officers and crews of the lost ships would, or could, make better the pains of starvation by cannibalism. Nobody can say that Franklin's men were not set upon and slain by the Eskimo themselves, because every savage is in his heart greedy, a liar, treacherous and cruel.

Adapted from Charles Dickens' article in "The Lost Artic Voyagers", published in 1854.

Look at the evidence

1   Look carefully at the map on p.154.

a) Sort the evidence on the map into:
- clues about what happened to the explorers
- information about the voyage.

b) Now group your evidence. Think about connections between the evidence. For example, think about evidence that suggests the explorers may have suffered from lead poisoning or food shortages.

Key words

Scurvy
A disease caused by a lack of vitamin C.

Tuberculosis
A lung disease, sometimes known as TB.

Use the source

2   Read **source b**.

a) What reasons does Charles Dickens give to explain why he thinks the explorers did not resort to cannibalism?

b) How useful do you think Dickens' views are in finding out what happened? Think about the 5Ws (see page 182) to help you answer this question.

Link it together

3   Weigh up all the evidence and explain what you think happened to the explorers of the Franklin expedition. Think about links between factors: do you think that more than one factor contributed to their deaths?
How did they contribute?

Escaping the Irish Famine

Source a is a painting of Irish people at the port in Liverpool in the 1840s. They are on their way to America. **Source b** shows life on board a ship sailing to America.

? *What do these pictures tell you?*
Describe five things you can see in each one.

■ *Irish people arriving in Liverpool on their way from Ireland to America, engraved in 1850.*

■ *An image from 1851 showing what life was like on board a ship taking Irish people to America.*

Why move?

Starting a new life in a new country is a big step for any family, yet many people move to different places around the world. This is often a big change for those who move, and some people find it hard to adapt to their new country. It was just the same in the nineteenth century; millions of people emigrated to start a new life abroad and experienced major problems.

People move for a number of reasons. These reasons can be divided into:

● push factors (which explain why people decide to leave somewhere)

● pull factors (which explain why people are attracted to a place).

Your turn ...

1 In pairs, read the ten cards opposite, which give reasons why people might move to another country. Then arrange them into 'push' and 'pull' factors. Explain to another pair or group how you came to your decision.

CARD 1
COMMUNITY

There were large communities of Irish people living in big cities in North America including Toronto and Ontario in Canada, and Boston and New York. They provided food and money for Irish people arriving in their cities.

CARD 2
YOUTH

Young people in particular could find work in America and could send money back to Ireland to help their relatives.

CARD 3
POTATOES

More than one-third of Irish people ate nothing but potatoes. From 1845 to 1849 the potato crop was destroyed by a fungus. Between 1845 and 1851 between 1.1 million and 1.5 million Irish people died of famine.

CARD 4
LAND

Most of the land in Ireland was owned by a small number of people. The large majority of Irish people had little chance of owning more than a tiny plot of land.

CARD 5
WORK

Lancashire and Yorkshire in England were attractive places to move to because there was plenty of work in the factories and fields.

CARD 6
TRANSPORT

Transport on ships (known as 'coffin ships') to America was very cheap. Getting to England was also cheap. In the 1840s it cost just half a penny to travel from Cork to London.

CARD 7
GOVERNMENT

In 1846 the British government tried to help the starving people in Ireland by providing work such as mending roads through public work schemes. In February 1847 the government set up around 600 soup kitchens but in late 1847 they were closed.

CARD 8
LANDLORDS

Some landlords were kind to their starving tenants giving them food and not making them pay their rents. Other landlords were not so kind, throwing their tenants out of their houses in what is known as 'eviction'.

CARD 9
RAILWAYS

Railways were being built across Britain and America in the 1840s. There was plenty of work for railways labourers, who became known as 'navvies'.

CARD 10
FOOD SUPPLY

The British government imported grain from Canada to help the starving. But rather than giving the grain away, the government sold it.

Consider the factors

2 **a)** Working in your pairs from task 1, order 'push' cards to reflect the most important reason people left Ireland (the least important reason should be at the bottom). Now do the same with your 'pull' cards.

b) Make a note of your lists, explaining why you chose the most important and least important 'push' and 'pull' factors.

In conclusion ...

3 Imagine you are an Irish person who has emigrated. Write a letter home to your relatives. In your letter you should include details about:

● why you left Ireland
● where you travelled to and how.

Use the information from the cards to help you write your letter.

You could also imagine what your new life is like and describe this to your family. Think about:

● how you are going to earn money
● how you feel about being in a new country.

History detective

Go to www. heinemann.co.uk/ hotlinks to find out more about Irish migration. Have a look at these sites and see if you can find any more sites on your own.

3.5b

Key words

Chieftain
Person in charge of a large Scottish family.

Croft
The house and land a Scottish family lived on and farmed.

The Highland Clearances

? *What can you see happening in this picture?*
Who do you think the people are? Why might this be happening?

What were the Highland Clearances?

Following victory at Culloden in 1746, the English wanted to reduce the power of the Highland **chieftains** and the Scottish clans.

⬇

The chieftains ruled over the Scottish clans. After losing to the English army at the Battle of Culloden in 1746, many chieftains became more interested in making money and pleasing their new English landlords than looking after their clans.

⬇

The Highlands of Scotland were home to the Scottish clans. They had farmed there for generations and made money from selling vegetables from their **crofts**. Life had stayed the same for years. The chieftains and English landlords wanted to use this land for grazing sheep, as it would make more money. The only problem was they did not want to pay the clans for their land; they decided to take it instead. Scottish clans living in the Highlands felt betrayed by their clan chieftains.

Make connections

1 Imagine you are a clan chieftain explaining to your family why you decided to work for the English instead of supporting your clan.

a) Write down what you would say to them. Try to include at least two reasons.

b) Look back at the explanation you have just written. Would a historian think this is a good enough reason for someone to betray their clan? Explain your answer.

How were the Highland Clearances carried out?

Clan chieftains and English landlords used many different tactics during the Highland Clearances. Look at the diagram below to find out about some of these.

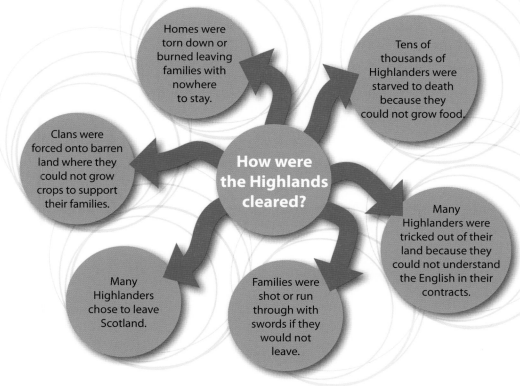

Homes were torn down or burned leaving families with nowhere to stay.

Tens of thousands of Highlanders were starved to death because they could not grow food.

Clans were forced onto barren land where they could not grow crops to support their families.

How were the Highlands cleared?

Many Highlanders were tricked out of their land because they could not understand the English in their contracts.

Many Highlanders chose to leave Scotland.

Families were shot or run through with swords if they would not leave.

Highland potato famine

The Highlands suffered a potato famine between 1846 and 1857, similar to the Irish potato famine of 1846. As in Ireland, many families suffered. Clan chiefs and English landlords did not try to help; instead they continued with the clearances. Many elderly people and children died from starvation. Scottish families were forced to leave the Highlands to look for work in larger towns such as Dundee, Glasgow and Edinburgh. Some Scottish families were so desperate they fled to England. As a result of the clearances, large areas of the Scottish Highlands remain uninhabited today.

Change points of view

2 Imagine you are a clan member in 1846. Use the information in this lesson to write a paragraph describing your experience during the Clearances.

3 Now imagine you are an English landlord. Use the same information to write a paragraph from this new point of view. Remember, as a landlord you won't think you are doing anything wrong!

Link it together

3 Read through this lesson and Lesson 3.5a. Working with a partner, make a list of the differences between how the Scottish were treated compared with the treatment of the Irish during their times of difficulties.

Remembering the Highland Clearances

The Highland Clearances were one of the worst tragedies in Scottish history. To ensure that the thousands killed during the Clearances are remembered, monuments and plaques have been put up for the public to see.

The statue shown in **source a** was built in 1834 in memory of the Duke of Sutherland. It stands overlooking the Highlands where his clans lived. It is one of the most famous monuments in Scotland.

The Duke of Sutherland

The Duke was the eldest son of the Marquess of Stafford and has been called the 'richest man of the nineteenth century', such was the amount of land and wealth he owned.

■ *This statue of the Duke of Sutherland was erected in 1834.*

b

The Duke of Sutherland died in 1833. One year after his death a monument was built on the top of Beinn mountain above Golspie. The dedication on the plaque says that the monument was built by 'a mourning and grateful tenantry' to a 'judicious, kind and liberal landlord'. The statue was paid for by clan family members still living on the Duke of Sutherland's estates who had not been forced to leave during the Clearances. However, the wording on the memorial plaque was not chosen by the people who paid for the statue, but by the Duke's family at the time of his death.

c

Patrick Sellar, who worked for the Duke of Sutherland, wrote at the time of the Clearances that Lord and Lady Stafford were 'pleased to order the new arrangement of this country'. He said that the people were to be 'brought down to the coast and placed in lots of less than 3 acres, just large enough to support an industrious family, but just small enough to cause them to turn their attention to the fishing. A most kind action, to put these barbarous Highlanders into a position where they could better live together, apply themselves to industry and educate their children.'

d

The Duke and Duchess of Sutherland had reputations for being the most hated couple in Highland history. Many clan members felt let down by them. The Duke of Sutherland forced a large number of his tenant farmers off his land and towards the coast in order to make money from sheep farming. At the height of the clearances almost 2,000 people were cleared off Sutherland land.

e

The Duchess of Sutherland was quoted as saying to a friend in England that 'Scotch people are of happier constitution, and do not fatten like the larger breed of animals'. She did not care for the well-being of the people who had lived on Sutherland for generations. She was particularly unsympathetic towards the starving and freezing families that were cleared from the land.

f

Donald Macleod was present when Rosal, one of the Highland townships, was cleared. He was an eyewitness of the scene and recalled that strong parties led by Sellar and Young (Sutherland's men) commenced 'setting fire to the dwellings until about 300 houses were in flames, the people striving to remove the sick, the helpless, before the fire should reach them. The cries of women and children, the roaring of cattle, the barking of dogs, the smoke of the fire, the soldiers – it required to be seen to be believed!'

g

When the Duke of Sutherland died it was his family and employees who encouraged the few clan members left on the Duke's land to pay for the monument. The monument was the idea of James Loch, the Sutherland Estate manager. He wanted to build the monument to 'preserve the memory of the Duke'. The monument cost £1,400 to build and records at the time show it was funded through public subscription. Many of the contributors were the same tenants who had been evicted from their land. Some clan members felt they had no choice but to pay for the statue because if they did not their relatives might also be cleared from the only home they had known.

Think it through

1 Why do you think monuments dedicated to events such as the Highland Clearances are built?

2 Why do you think the Duke of Sutherland was chosen as the person to go on the top of the monument in **source a**? Work in pairs to suggest reasons.

3 Read through boxes b–g. What impression do you have now of the Duke of Sutherland? Think back to the answer you gave in task 2. Do you feel that your answer was accurate?

4 In 1995 many residents of Golspie in the Scottish Highlands asked for the Sutherland monument to be pulled down. They wanted an appropriate monument to the Highland Clearance victims to be built instead.

    a) Do you agree with the residents of Golspie that the Sutherland Monument should be pulled down? Why? Use information from these pages to support your answer.

    b) Now write a letter to the local council either supporting or arguing against the plans of the residents of Golspie to build a more appropriate monument.

5 You have been asked to design a more appropriate monument that could be built to remember the victims of the Highland Clearances. Think about the type of monument you would build. Would it include a statue? If so, of what? If not, what might it look like? Go to www.heinemann.co.uk/hotlinks for further research and ideas.

next lesson

What was the impact of steam on transport?

In this lesson you will:

- find out what life was like on board a sailing ship
- identify advantages and disadvantages of sailing ships.

Life at sea

The East Indiamen

In the eighteenth century a lot of money could be made from trading with India and the Far East. Specially designed sailing ships were built for the task. They were called East Indiamen and they were the largest merchant ships at the time.

■ *An East Indiaman painted in 1795.*

? *Look at this picture. What do you think are the five most important features about East Indiaman ships?*

Key features of an East Indiaman

Below are the key features of an East Indiaman.

A	The huge hold was used to store large amounts of valuable cargo.
B	A voyage only cost what it took to pay the sailors and provide them with food. The ship used wind power, which was free!
C	Such large ships required a large crew, often as many as 100 men.
D	Conditions on board were cramped. Men slept in hammocks, often with only 40cm between each hammock.
E	Sails needed to be put up and down depending on the strength of the wind and to vary the speed of the ship. Going up the rigging could be very dangerous, and many men were lost overboard this way.
F	East Indiamen appeared to have two decks of guns, although usually not all the weapons were fitted. This was to protect the ships and their cargoes from attacks by pirates.
G	A return voyage to the Far East could take more than a year if the winds were not favourable.
H	Long voyages increased the risk of disease among the crew. Scurvy was common on long voyages, caused by a lack of the vitamins found in fresh fruit and vegetables.

| **I** | The death rate on ships taking more than eight months to sail to the East Indies and back was four times as high as those that returned in a shorter time. |

| **J** | A typical sailors' diet included 1 pound of boiled salted beef three days a week for dinner, and a pudding made of flour and suet. On two other days they ate boiled salted pork with a pudding of dried peas. On the remaining days they had pea soup and salted fish. |

| **K** | Life on board was very hard work because a sailing ship took a lot of skill and effort to sail. |

| **L** | Sailors on East Indiamen were paid well, receiving £20 for a voyage and the owners of the ships could make huge profits by selling the valuable cargo in Britain. |

Finding a crew

Because sailing ships required such large crews to sail them and because life on board was tough, men were sometimes forced into the navy. This was especially true in times of war when even more sailors were needed. Groups of sailors, called Press Gangs, went around towns kidnapping boys and men and forced them to work on the ships.

As I was crossing Towerhill I was accosted by a person in seamen's dress who tapped me on the shoulder and asked 'What ship are you with?' I replied, with surprise, that he must be mistaken as I was not a sailor. The fellow then gave a whistle and in a moment I was in the hands of six or eight ruffians who I immediately dreaded, and soon found out to be, a press gang.

■ *William Hay's account of being forced into the navy by a press gang, 1744.*

Think about it

1. Read boxes A–L. Sort these statements into the advantages and disadvantages of East Indiamen.
   - Think first from the point of view of a company that owned such a ship and sold the cargo it brought back from the Far East.
   - Now think about it from the point of view of a sailor on an East Indiaman. What changes have you made to your sorting?
2. Imagine you are a sailor. Use your sorting in task 1 to decide the top three criticisms of an East Indiaman sailing ship.

Consider the information

3. One of the disadvantages of the East Indiamen was that they relied on the wind to power them.
   a) How might relying on wind power affect the following:
   - the comfort and conditions on board the ship.
   - the profits that could be made through trade.
   b) What problems facing the East Indiamen when travelling to the Far East had nothing to do with them being sailing ships?

In conclusion ...

4. Write a letter to the owner of a company that specialises in buying ships to trade with the Far East. Persuade the owner to invest money in new 'steam' technology so that ships might not have to rely on the power of the wind for movement in the future.

In this lesson you will:

- understand the advantages of the invention of steam ships

- identify the impact of steam ships in the nineteenth century.

Steam versus sail

Wind power or steam power?

From the 1800s, more and more ships were fitted with steam engines. Steam-powered ships seemed to have many advantages over sailing ships.

Journey times could be predicted more accurately, making passenger services possible. For example, in London steam ships began to travel up and down the Thames taking commuters to work.

They could carry more passengers than stagecoaches, so charged less and offered more spacious accommodation. The cost of a journey between London and Edinburgh on a steamer in 1825 was £2 including meals, while a stagecoach cost £4 10s.

The advantages of steam ships

Speed and direction were less affected by wind and tides.

Luxury travel became possible. P&O steam ships operated a regular service to Spain and Portugal from the 1830s.

Factfile

A record of steamship accidents

1845

Three men in small boats were drowned by the wash from two steamers (the *Eclipse* and the *Prince of Wales*) when both ships were travelling at full speed.

27 August 1847

The steamer the *Cricket* exploded killing seventeen passengers and injuring nearly 60. It was later found that the safety valve on the boiler had been illegally tied down to increase pressure and therefore increase speed.

September 1878

The passenger steamer the *Princess Alice* collided with a steam ship transporting coal on the Thames. The *Princess Alice* was carrying 900 passengers on a daytrip to Margate and more than 550 of them were drowned.

Your turn ...

1   Design an advertisement for a new steam boat passenger service, highlighting the advantages of travel by steam ships.

Did steam mean the end of sail?

Although steam ships quickly replaced sailing ships on passenger services, sailing ships were still used to carry cargo to and from Asia. Steam ships had disadvantages on such long routes.

- They needed huge amounts of coal, which meant less space for cargo. Coal was also expensive.

- If the ships could not carry enough coal on board they would have to stop to refuel.

There were also concerns about the safety of the new ships.

Think about it!

2   What evidence can you find in the information on this page to suggest that not everyone would have supported the introduction of steam ships?

Clipper ships

In the 1850s a new type of fast sailing ship, the clipper, was designed to transport goods to and from Asia. Clippers were very fast because they used the strong **trade winds**. In 1854 a clipper crossed the Atlantic in twelve days – three days faster than the quickest steam ship at the time. They could also carry a lot of cargo because no space was taken up by coal or engines. On its first voyage, the *Cutty Sark* carried a massive 1,450 tonnes of tea.

Steam takes over

By 1878 the clippers were no longer needed. The Suez Canal opened in 1869 linking the Mediterranean Sea with the Red Sea. This shortened the distance from London to Bombay (Mumbai as it is now) by over 7,000km, because ships no longer had to sail around Africa.

Sailing ships were unable to use the Suez Canal because the trade winds they relied on did not blow in that direction. The Suez Canal meant that steam ships, which were becoming safer and more efficient, could take over.

Key words

Trade winds
These winds, which sweep across the ocean, were relied on by sail ships to complete their journey as quickly as possible.

Consider the information

3 Look at the information in this lesson.

a) Which type of ship would you choose for each of the journeys below, before the Suez Canal was built? Give reasons for your choices.

- A tourist passenger boat service on the River Clyde in Scotland.
- To transport tea from China.
- To transport milk from Holland.
- To transport wool from Australia.
- A passenger service between Britain and America.

b) Which of your answers would you change if you were completing the information in 1869 after the Suez Canal had been built? Why?

Did you know?

The first steamship to sail between America and Britain in 1819, the SS *Savannah*, used the engines for only 3½ days of the 27 day voyage, relying on sail power for most of the journey.

In conclusion ...

4 Which of the following statements would you agree with and why?

Statement 1: The invention of the steam ship in the 1800s was a turning point (a dramatic and immediate change) in water transport.

Statement 2: The invention of the steam ship in the 1800s did not lead to any real change in water transport until the building of the Suez Canal in 1869.

Statement 3: The invention of the steam ship in the 1800s was a very significant change in water transport, although its full effects were not seen until after the Suez Canal was built in 1869.

In this lesson you will:

- identify reasons for the development of an alternative form of transport in the nineteenth century

- assess the nature of change that happened to Victorian business because of the growth of the railways.

Why the railways?

Transporter beam invented!

No longer the stuff of science-fiction, scientists today unveiled a revolutionary way of transporting material by 'beaming' it to another location.

? *If this was a real headline what changes would it bring about in the way we live and work? What problems would there be for those who transport things around the country today?*

River and road transport

For centuries people travelled around Britain either by boat or the rivers or by foot or horse. Both had their problems.

I wish I didn't have to use the local river to move my goods. There are always problems depending on the season. It's better with the canals but even they have their difficulties for a farming business like mine.

At least you don't have to use the roads for your goods. The surface is often little more than a narrow, dangerous dirt track in places. It can be a nightmare if you want to get anywhere fast.

Your turn ...

1 With a partner, think about the transport problems the two villagers had during different times of the year. Then copy and complete the table below.

	Spring	Summer	Autumn	Winter
River				
Canal				
Road				

? *What other reasons might there be for wanting to use a railway rather than canals or the roads?*

Did you know?

In 1804 an early railway locomotive made by Richard Trevithick was so heavy it broke the rails it was running on.

Transporting by rail

As Britain began to develop towns and factories, more people needed to transport goods reliably and quickly. With the invention of the steam engine the idea of moving goods by railway became a possibility.

During the 1820s businessmen began to look into building a rail link between the port of Liverpool and the city of Manchester – two of the largest cities in Britain at the time. Raw cotton that landed at Liverpool's docks took 20 hours to be transported by canal to the mills of Manchester.

However the new railway would be a huge risk because it would be very expensive to build.

Over to you ...

2 Imagine you are the chairperson of a company that wants to build the first railway in your area. A local business person, who you have approached to invest in your scheme, asks you these questions.

- Who will use the railway?
- Why do they need it?
- What would they use it for?
- When will they use it?
- How will I benefit from it?

a) With a partner list answers that would convince the business person to invest.

b) The business person is still not convinced. What other questions might they ask you before deciding to invest in the company?

The advantages of rail

One of the biggest advantages of the railway was that it was so much faster than other forms of transport and could carry more weight. People could also make a lot of money from it.

The Liverpool to Manchester line was completed in 1830 and to begin with just the owners wanted to use the railways to transport goods between cities. However, it soon seemed that everyone wanted to travel by rail. In 1835 Britain had only 544 kilometres of track, but by 1900 there were 30,000 kilometres carrying 1.1 million passengers and 419 million tonnes of freight.

Tell the story

3 It is 1837 and you are a reporter for your local newspaper. You are to write a report about the proposed new railway. Include in your report the problems which businesses currently face and how the railway will help solve them.

Impact of the railways

Imagine that you are travelling today from London, but that your journey time is 6 hours to get to Oxford, 15 hours to Birmingham, and 46 hours to Edinburgh!

? *What things might not be possible as a result of having such long journey times?*

During the nineteenth century, the railway developed from a new form of transport to something the whole country depended on. As it developed, the use of the railway began to change and people's reactions to the railways also changed over time.

■ *Trains compete for the right to be the first inter-city locomotive, Rainhill, 1829.*

■ *'Catch-Me-Who-Can' at Euston, London, 1808.*

■ *Charing Cross station, London, in 1900.*

■ *Passengers being transported in the 1840s.*

Think about it

1 Using **sources a–d** to help you, what do you think people's attitudes towards the railways would have been at different points during the nineteenth century? Share your ideas with a partner.

Building the railways

There were no heavy cutting and lifting machines at the time so all the building work had to be done by hand and moved by horses. The railways provided many other jobs for people in the town, as well as giving opportunities for cheap travel to many who had only been able to visit other places on special occasions.

Over to you ...

2 a) Using **sources a–d**, which of the following statements do you most agree with? Give two reasons for your choice.

Statement 1: The railway was always a popular form of transport.

Statement 2: The railway was only popular towards the end of the nineteenth century.

Statement 3: The railway was popular because it was a flexible form of transport.

Statement 4: The railway changed Britain.

b) In groups of three, share your answers. Between you, decide which you think is the most accurate statement and identify three reasons why. Share your conclusions with other groups in your class.

c) In the light of your class discussion, write another statement that you believe to be true. Give supporting reasons.

Not everyone was happy with the railway's arrival in their town. Some people were fearful of the ways in which their traditional life might change. Others were concerned about the construction itself. Companies who built the railways employed huge numbers of men ('navvies') to do the work. The arrival in a town of these hard-working, hard-drinking men was greeted with alarm by some locals.

Impact of the railway

A Soldiers could travel from Manchester to Liverpool in two hours rather than a full day's march.

B Cheap third-class tickets allowed working-class people to travel.

C To travel by railway was half the cost of a stage coach.

D Goods that would go off (milk, vegetables) could be transported further than before.

E Heavy goods (such as coal) could be carried ten times faster than by canal for two-thirds the price.

F Railways were safe to travel on after dark.

G Goods were less likely to be stolen from a railway than from a canal.

H The newspapers reported that there were few problems with smoke or noise from those who lived by the railway.

In conclusion ...

3 Give each point (A–H) a number to show how big a change you think the railways had on the lives of ordinary people. (1 = the biggest impact; 8 = the smallest.)

4 Compare your list with a partner.

a) What are the similarities and differences between your lists?

b) What basis did you use to make your list? What basis did your partner use?

c) Combine your two lists into one. Then give clear reasons why you have ordered your new list in this way.

5 Later in the century people began to use the railways for different things, such as:

- transporting and distributing national newspapers
- going to exhibitions – like the Great Exhibition in London
- going on holiday to seaside resorts like Blackpool.

Replace three of the uses on your list with these new uses. Then reorder these points. Explain your reasons for your new list.

In this lesson you will:

■ find out about the importance of India to the British Empire

■ assess the impact of the British Empire on India.

Key words

Ceylon
Small island off the southern tip of India. Now known as Sri Lanka.

Native
Term used in Victorian society to describe people in the colonies. It suggests they need to be 'civilised'.

Viceroy
British governor of a colony.

Did you know?

Queen Victoria ruled over the British Empire but she never left Europe. Instead she put **viceroys** in post to represent her in the colonies and report back to her.

Jewel in the crown: a very British India?

? **What British influences can you see?**

■ *A photograph showing Calcutta around 1900.*

The British in India

In the eighteenth century, India was ruled by emperors known as *mughals*. Each district of India was ruled by *nawabs* and *rajahs* (princes) who had as much power as a king. The mughals allowed European traders to set up factories along the coast.

By 1750 the main westerners in India were the British and the French who would take opposite sides in quarrels among the nawabs and rajahs. By 1757 the British had asserted their superiority and, with the India Act of 1784, Britain formally claimed authority over India.

The East India Company employed the British in India, paid for the soldiers, had its own officers, and began to give protection to the districts of the nawabs and the rajahs. As the company took over each district it collected taxes and kept law and order. By 1850 the East India Company controlled most of India either directly or through its protection services.

b Let us visit … the Hill Club at Nuwara Eliya in **Ceylon**. This little town lay high among the tea estates. The British have laid out a park with a maze and a botanical garden. They had dammed a little lake. They had marked out gentle walks around the surrounding woods. There was a big half-timbered grand hotel and a cottage for the Governor of Ceylon with a pond and croquet lawn. There was the inevitable golf and race course. There were villas strung about the lake, an English church and a lending library.

■ *Extract from James Morris'* Pax Britannica, *published in 1968.*

Report back

1 a) Study **sources a** and **b**. Note down:
   - any British influences
   - any Indian influences.

   b) Use this information to write a report from India to Queen Victoria. Describe what India looks like under British rule and how it is truly a 'British India'.

■ Indian workers in 1880 loading raw cotton onto ships to be made into cloth in Britain.

d
I hate the British for the wrong they have done in India. Their parliament makes laws for us and their government appoints a viceroy to rule over us. The British are arrogant, despising our brown skins. Worst of all, the British have kept us poor. Our people toil for slave wages in British-owned cotton mills and on British tea plantations.

■ The view of Pandit Jawaharlal Nehru, who became India's prime minister after Indian independence in 1947.

Use the sources

2 According to Queen Victoria the aim of the British Empire was to 'protect the poor **natives** and to advance civilisation'. Using **sources a–d**, complete a table like the one below to analyse if it achieved those aims in India.

Evidence that the British did 'protect the poor natives and advance civilisation'	Evidence that the British did not 'protect the poor natives and advance civilisation'

■ A British cotton factory in 1860. Workers here made the Indian raw cotton into cotton thread.

What are the similarities?

3 Compare and contrast **sources c** and **e**. Fill in the thought bubbles of the Indian worker and the British worker. What similar thoughts would they have had about:
   - working conditions/treatment
   - wages/poverty
   - the riches produced by cotton?

4 By looking at the similarities in experiece of the workers in Britain and in Britain's Indian colony, how far would an observer be right in saying that Britain created a very British India?

3.7b

- find out what caused the 'Indian Mutiny' and how the incident has been portrayed in history

- understand that interpretations reflect the circumstances and principles of the time in which they were made.

Key words

Mutiny
An uprising against lawful rule.

Sepoys
Indian soldiers paid for by the British East India Company.

The bullet that started a 'mutiny'

? *What do you think source a is showing?*

Tensions between the British and the Indians came to a head in 1857 when the British introduced a new type of rifle. But the **sepoys** did not want to use the new rifles because they were told to grease the cartridges with cow or pig fat. This would have been offensive to many sepoys who were either Hindu or Muslim. Cows are sacred to Hindus and Muslims do not eat or use anything that comes from a pig.

However, the greased cartridges were just one reason why there was an 'Indian **Mutiny**'. The list below gives you some more reasons.

Causes of the 'Indian Mutiny'

- Fear that traditional Indian religions would be taken over by the missionaries and their Christian religion.

- A rebellion of soldiers against their officers.

- British trade was ruining Indian trade.

- No Indians were employed in senior jobs such as judges or army officers.

- The British did not respect or understand Indian ways.

- It was an opportunity to rebel against a foreign ruler.

- The British simply wanted to build an empire to increase power. They thought they were superior to the Indians.

Your turn ...

1 Use the list opposite to complete a table like the one below. Make suggestions about how each cause could have contributed to the 'Indian Mutiny'. Then number the causes in order of importance in your opinion.

Cause of the 'Indian Mutiny'	Why would this cause the 'Mutiny'?	Order of importance

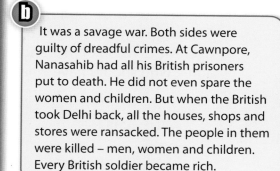

b It was a savage war. Both sides were guilty of dreadful crimes. At Cawnpore, Nanasahib had all his British prisoners put to death. He did not even spare the women and children. But when the British took Delhi back, all the houses, shops and stores were ransacked. The people in them were killed – men, women and children. Every British soldier became rich.

■ *Adapted from a book by the Indian historian D. P. Singhal, published in 1983.*

c If I told you about all the things the rebels have done you would not believe me. Such awful crimes have never been known before. You in England will not hear the worst, for the worst is so bad that the papers would not dare publish. The British soldiers here are furious. They say very little, but every face shows that when the time comes they will show no mercy to those who have shown themselves.

■ *Letter from a journalist in India to an English newspaper, 1857.*

What do the sources tell us?

2 Read **sources b** and **c**, which both describe the 'Indian Mutiny'.

  a) What similarities are there about conditions during the 'Mutiny'?

  b) What differences do the sources describe about who caused such conditions?

  c) Look at the attribution of the sources. Why are the sources so different?

After two years of fighting, the 'Indian Mutiny' was eventually over. The 'Mutiny' had failed. The Government of India Act was passed in 1858, ending the rule of the East India Company. Power passed to a new India Department and a British viceroy. The number of British soldiers in India was increased.

In conclusion ...

3 **Source c** is a piece of propaganda.

  a) Why would the British print such an article in a newspaper?

  b) Is a piece of propaganda still a useful piece of evidence to a historian of this period? Explain your answer.

4 If you look in most history books this incident is called the 'Indian Mutiny', even today.

  a) What relationship does this title suggest between India and Britain?

  b) Is this an appropriate name for the incident? Why?

  c) What title could you give the incident that was not problematic in this way?

3.7c

In this lesson you will:

■ investigate the significant events of the 'Scramble for Africa' and consider how they illustrate changing attitudes towards empire

■ understand features of past societies in a chronological framework.

The Scramble for Africa

The period 1870–1914 is known as the 'Scramble for Africa'. When major European powers such as Britain, Belgium, France and Germany argued over the division of the lands of Africa. These powers held conferences to agree who should have what, but this did not prevent war.

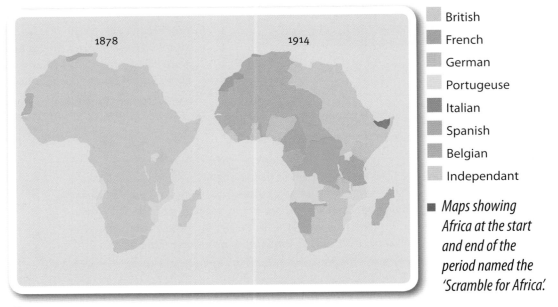

| British |
| French |
| German |
| Portugeuse |
| Italian |
| Spanish |
| Belgian |
| Independant |

■ *Maps showing Africa at the start and end of the period named the 'Scramble for Africa'.*

Use the map

1 Look carefully at the maps. Compare how Africa was divided between the European powers at the start and end of the period labelled the 'Scramble for Africa'. Describe to a partner how the distribution of power has changed. Pay particular attention to whole areas controlled by one power and how they are spread across Africa.

Egypt

In 1878 Egypt, in north-east Africa, was bankrupt and under the control of the Turkish Empire. The British, in partnership with the French, gave Egypt financial help. To accept the help the Egyptians also had to accept restrictions on their own trade and economy, which led to suffering and uprisings. When Englishmen were killed in riots in Alexandria, the Royal Navy shelled the city. The British decided to **annex** Egypt without discussion with France and ordered land and sea forces to take control.

a A few years ago, our government and the French began to interfere in Egypt, without having any right to do so. The result was that the National Party was formed. Its slogan was 'Egypt for the Egyptians'. If Englishmen cried 'England for the English' we would praise them. So why should we condemn Egyptians for doing the same?

■ *From a report of a meeting of the Workmen's Peace Association, 24 June 1882.*

b At last the world has been taught what happens if England is defied and its subjects were killed. In fact, what has happened was good for both Egypt and for England. Egypt has been freed from the rule of the National Party tyrants. And the massacre of Englishmen has been avenged.

■ *Adapted from a report in The Observer newspaper, 16 July 1882.*

Use the sources

2 Read **sources a** and **b**, then answer the questions below.

a) What do both authors feel about the behaviour of the Egyptians and the British reaction to it?

b) How does **source a** show a change in British attitude for some towards the empire? Explain your answer using specific information from the source.

c) How does **source b** show how some British attitudes towards the empire remained the same? Explain your answer using specific information from the source.

c

■ *The British fought the Boer War in southern Africa between 1899 and 1902.*

The Boer War

During the second half of the nineteenth century the British controlled parts of Southern Africa and had agreed that the Dutch could have semi-independent control of the Orange Free State and Transvaal. Up to 1886 they were happy with this situation. However, in 1886 gold was discovered in Transvaal, and many British moved into the area to take advantage and exploit the gold reserves. News soon travelled that these British settlers were being denied political rights. So the British began to move more soldiers into the area. They were determined to show the **Boers** that they were the superior nation and to take control of such an increasingly wealthy area. At first British support for the war was strong and many men volunteered to fight. However, this support was short-lived. Source d explains how the war progressed before a peace treaty was signed in 1902 in which the Boers came, briefly under British rule.

Key words

Annex
When a country gains new land.

Boer
Dutch settlers who lived in Southern Africa.

d

The later stages of the war were not glorious at all but involved brutal methods used against Boer forces. The British under Lord Kitchener laid waste large stretches of Boer land to deprive fighters of cover and support and herded many families into concentration camps where almost 30,000 died. The country (Britain) was too easily criticised as bullying and showing none of that famous sense of 'fair play', which was supposed to be bred into Christian English gentlemen.

■ *Extract from Eric Evans' The Birth of Modern Britain, published in 1997.*

In conclusion ...

3 Think back to the reasons the British gave for expanding the empire at the start of this enquiry: 'to civilise the natives' and 'spread the Christian religion'. According to **source d** did British actions in the Boer War reflect these aims? Explain your answer using details from the source.

4 Interestingly only small numbers of British men from industrial towns who volunteered to fight in the Boer War were classed as unfit for service due to poor health. Many of those who were accepted to fight were not at full health. How do you think this would have affected British opinion about continuing to expand the empire?

3.7d

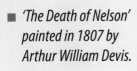

A heroic death?

? *What is shown in this picture?*
Do you know its name?
What was it built to celebrate?

Horatio Nelson was the famous admiral in charge of the British fleet at the Battle of Trafalgar in 1805, when the British won against the French and Spanish fleets. Nelson first joined the navy when he was 12 years old in 1771, and by the age of 20 he had become the youngest captain in the Royal Navy.

Nelson was a brave commander. He was blinded in his right eye when he was hit by **shrapnel** from French guns in 1794. Then, in a battle against the Spanish, he lost his right arm when it was shattered by a **musket ball**. He led the British navy to victory many times and was celebrated as a hero in his own lifetime.

Nelson was fatally injured during the Battle of Trafalgar, 1805, when he was shot from the rigging of a French ship. Nelson was taken to the cabin of his ship HMS *Victory* where he died, but not before learning that the British had won.

Key words

Musket ball
A lead ball fired from a gun.

Shrapnel
Fragments thrown out by an explosion.

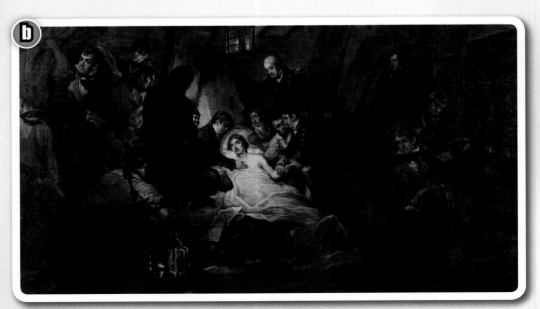

■ *'The Death of Nelson' painted in 1807 by Arthur William Devis.*

Information about the paintings

Source b: Arthur Devis carefully researched his painting of the death of Nelson. He read the account of Nelson's death by Nelson's surgeon William Beatty, who was there at the time. Devis also went on board HMS *Victory* to make sketches of the cabin of the ship where Nelson died.

Source d: The artist Benjamin West was not so concerned with accuracy. He described what he felt to be more important in **source c**.

c Nelson should not be represented as dying in the gloomy hold of a ship, like a sick man in a prison hole. No boy would be animated by a representation of Nelson dying like an ordinary man. His feelings must be roused and his mind inflamed by a scene great and extraordinary.

■ *The artist Benjamin West criticising Arthur Devis' painting 'The Death of Nelson' in 1808.*

Work it out!

1 Compare the paintings in **sources b** and **d** by copying and completing the table below.

	Source b	Source d
Where is Nelson shown as dying?		
Roughly how many people are shown around him? What are they doing?		
What is Nelson wearing?		
How does Nelson appear? What is he doing?		

2 Which painting (**source b** or **d**) do you think is a more accurate representation of the death of Nelson? Why?

3 Select some of the ways in which, by changing what really happened, the artist of **source d** makes Nelson's death seem more dramatic and heroic. Why do you think the artist deliberately changed some aspects of what really happened at Nelson's death in his painting?

■ *'The Death of Nelson' painted in 1806 by Benjamin West.*

Why did the ability of people to move and travel change the way they lived?

Look back at the lessons that you have covered in this unit. Each lesson described how people were moving and travelling, although where to and how far they went depended on many things.

As people travelled they had an effect on the people and places around them. For some the effect was small and only felt in the local area, for others their movement had worldwide consequences.

What's the impact?

1 Use the diagram on this page to look again at the lessons you have covered.

With a partner decide whether the people that moved in each lesson would have had an effect just in the local area, on the nation as a whole or internationally. Quickly make a list of what you decide, and then share your answers with another pair? Which ones do you agree on and which do you disagree on? How could you find out who was right?

International effects

National effects

Local effects

People did not all move to other places for the same reason. For many there were factors that were new to the age that affected the decision to travel. Also not everybody chose to travel. Some were forced into moving by others.

Some of the factors listed below played a part in why people moved during this period.

Cause and consequence

2 **a)** Look at the list you created with your partner in task 1 and then link each item on your list with the factors that cause travelling below.

   b) Can you see any links between the factors that cause travelling and the scale of the effect; i.e. whether it was local, national or international?

   c) Which other factors do you think could be added to the ones below?

Factors

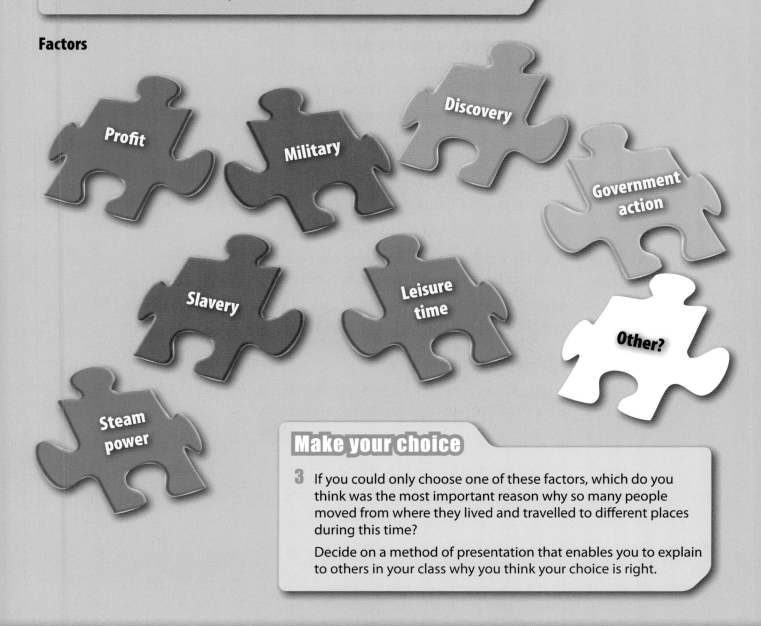

Make your choice

3 If you could only choose one of these factors, which do you think was the most important reason why so many people moved from where they lived and travelled to different places during this time?

   Decide on a method of presentation that enables you to explain to others in your class why you think your choice is right.

How had travel changed the world by 1901?

Standing in front of the time machine that brought you to 1901, you see that the numbers in the window now read 1603.

During your visit, you have seen many images, artefacts and documents about the changes in travel that had occured between 1603–1901. However you can only carry five things back in time with you that will help you explain to people how being able to move and travel more easily will change the world.

You now need to decide which five things made the most impact on how people travelled since 1603 and why they were so important.

How are you going to decide?

Look back over the lessons you have completed in this unit on moving and travelling:

For each lesson you'll need to look at the changes and write down the following:

- the title of the lesson
- where these changes happened – whether they were local, national or international
- what happened to the people involved
- how different people's lives were because of this change – very different, different, not very different
- how important these changes were? Give the change a score between 1 and 10, with 1 being very important
- you can also add a reference to an image from the lesson to help explain your point.

Lesson title

3.4a Cooks voyages of discovery

Circle where these changes happened

locally / nationally / (internationally)

What was the key point
What happened to the people in this lesson?

Accurate maps were made of parts of the world that hadn't been found by Europeans before. It meant other people from Britain could find their way back there easily.

Circle how different life was for people as a result of the changes that happened

very different / (different) / not very

How important were these changes?

(scale between 1–10, with 1 being very important)

1	2	3	4	5	6	7	8	9	10

Place the cards in a line in order of significance – those events that you feel produced the most significant changes on the right and those you think were less significant on the left.

Compare your line with those of other members of your group. Explain to them how you ordered the statements and how you reached a decision on where to place the events. Revise your own list if you need to.

Remember in the end you can only take five things back with you, so you need to be able to take the most significant ones.

How will your work be marked?
Have you:

Level 4
Been able to describe some features of the period?

Said that they are important?

Identified a reason why change happened and a consequence of that change?

Level 5
Been able to describe some of the main features of the period?

Begun to be aware of why some events, people and changes might be judged as more significant than others?

Been able to use selected information to explain why events or people were important?

Selected and used appropriate historical words to support and structure your work?

Level 6
Begun to show that you understand why conclusions about the importance of events, people and changes have been made?

Explained the way those conclusions have been reached?

Selected, organised and used relevant information, using the right historical words to produce structured work?

Use this section to remind yourself of some important historical skills. These hints will be useful as you complete the tasks and activities in this book.

Being a historian

These are some of the things that a historian does.

- Tells the story of the past.
- Explains why things happened and the consequences.
- Shows that some things change while others stay the same.
- Identifies why certain events and people are important.
- Works as a detective using evidence.
- Communicates about the past.
- Explains why interpretations differ.

Throughout this course you will have the chance to practise and improve all of these skills. Read through the descriptions below to find out what kind of historian you are.

Level 4 You can:

- tell the story of the past quite well
- give some reasons why events happen
- describe how some things have changed but others stay the same
- show how the past can be looked at in different ways
- use evidence to explain the past
- use the right words to explain the past.

Level 5 You can:

- tell the story of the past
- begin to explain why things happen
- explain how some things change while others stay the same
- begin to explain why some events and people are really important
- begin to ask questions of evidence
- use the right information to explain the past.

Level 6 You can:

- tell and explain the story of the past
- begin to explain how causes link together
- explain in detail why some things change and others stay the same
- ask questions why some people or events are more important than others
- decide which evidence i s useful
- use the right information and organise ideas clearly.

Evaluating a source

Evaluating a source means looking at it (or reading it) carefully and asking questions about it so that you can decide how valuable it is to a historian. Whatever the source, whether it's a diary or a letter, a photograph or a painting, you need to think about its nature (what it is), its origin (when and where it comes from, who it is by) and its purpose (why it was made). Use the 5×W rule to help you remember key questions to ask about the nature, origin and purpose of a source.

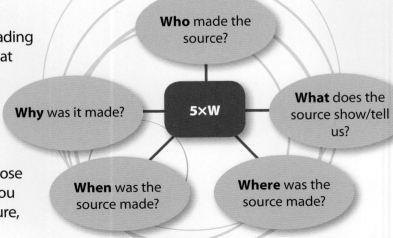

How and why do impressions differ?

Historians use pieces of evidence from many different sources. Sometimes the evidence will give different impressions or interpretations of the same event or person. This is something that the historian must think about before deciding which source to use.

Here are two written sources. You saw them first in Lesson 3.7a when you were finding out about British rule in India. They both describe the impact of British rule in India. You are going to read the sources again. After you have read the sources you are going to be asked 'How do these sources differ in their views of the British in India?'

Source a

Source a is from a book called *Pax Britannica*. The book was written by a British author James Morris in the 1960s and was published in 1968. In the book Morris describes the British Empire as he imagined it was like in 1900. It is not known whether James Morris visited Ceylon (now Sri Lanka).

a Let us visit…the Hill Club at Nuwara Eliya in Ceylon. This little town among the tea estates. The British have laid out a park with a maze and a botanical garden. They have dammed a little lake. They had marked out gentle walks around the surrounding woods. There was a big half-timbered grand hotel and a cottage for the Governor of Ceylon with a pond and a croquet lawn. There was the inevitable golf and race course. There were villas strung about the lake, an English church (of course) and a lending library.

Source b

Source b is from a speech made in 1942 by Pandit Jawaharlal Nehru. Nehru was an Indian nationalist which means that he did not like British rule in India.

b I hate the British for the wrong they have done in India. Their parliament makes laws for us and their government appoints a viceroy to rule over us. The British are arrogant, despising our brown skins. Worst of all, the British have kept us poor. Our people toil for slave wages in British-owned cotton mills and on British tea plantations.

How do these sources differ in their views of the British in India?

When answering this question you need to explain the differences in:

- **content**: what the sources actually say and the impression they give

- **tone**: how the sources sound; for example is the author positive or negative, angry or sad, happy or annoyed?

Here is the framework of two sentences to help you start an answer to the question. Fill in the gaps and the finish off the answer.

One way in which the sources differ is that source a gives the impression that the British improved …

However, source b gives the impression that the British made…

Another way in which the sources differ is that source a gives the impression that in the tea estates the British created …

But source b focuses on the fact that Indians worked on tea plantations for…

The next step is for you to explain why the two sources differ. This is where the 5xW can help. Compare the sources with each of the 5xW in mind. This is an example of the type of sentences you could write when considering who made the source.

The sources differ because the authors come from different backgrounds. The author of source b is an Indian nationalist who hated the British. It is not surprising that he has a different view from the British author of source a.

Your turn...

1. Using the advice above answer the following question: how and why do **sources a** and **b** differ in the impression they give about the impact of British rule in India?

Exploding a picture

Pictures can provide really useful evidence for historians. Sometimes they tell us far more than the artist intended them to. Sometimes they lead us to ask more and more questions so that the picture turns into a puzzle.

Look at this painting. You first saw it in Lesson 3.7d, when you were finding out about the death of Admiral Nelson. The British victory at the Battle of Trafalgar was very important and Nelson was a national hero. There were no cameras or camcorders at the start of the nineteenth century so paintings were one of the best ways in which Nelson's death could be described. But we have to be careful and ask a number of questions before we accept the painting as being useful evidence.

First think about the artist. This is called looking at the provenance or origin of the painting. Remember the **5×W** rule!

- Who painted the picture?
- When did they paint it?
- Was he (or she) there at the time?
- Were they in a good position to know what was going on, or did they make it up afterwards?
- Why did he (or she) paint the picture?
- Did someone pay them to do it?
- Were they trying to make a particular point?

You won't find answers to all these questions for every picture you look at, but you need to bear them in mind and answer the ones you can. This will help you sort out whether a picture is giving you accurate evidence of what happened at the time, or not.

Now look at the picture itself. This one is called 'The Death of Nelson'.

- What can you see in the middle of the painting?
- What is happening around the death scene?
- How is Nelson portrayed?

This is what the artist set out to show.

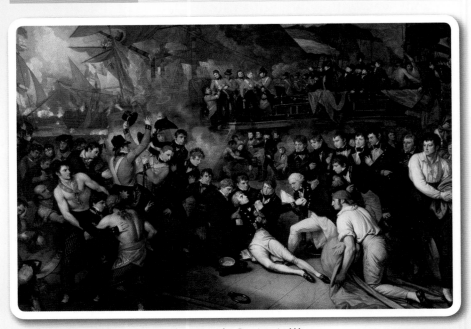

■ *'The Death of Nelson' painted in 1806 by Benjamin West.*

There are other things in the painting that the artist did not set out to show but which tell us a lot about, in this case, the early nineteenth century. This is called 'unwitting testimony'. Look carefully at the painting.

- What does it tell you about attitudes towards Nelson?
- How sea battles were fought?
- Fighting ships?
- Uniforms and clothes?
- The people who took part in the battle?

Finally check what you can see in the painting against what you know about life at sea at the time.

Do you think this painting can be considered reliable evidence of the death of Nelson? **Why? Why not?**

Unpacking a written source

Remember the **5×W** rule! This applies as much to written sources as it does to pictures and paintings.

Read through these two sources. They come from the book *The Interesting Narrative of the Life of Olaudah Equiano*, or *Gustavus Vassa the African*, which was published in 1789. The book was written by Olaudah Equiano who had been a slave in the Americas.

c
I now wished for death, but soon two of the white men offered me food; and, on refusing to eat, one of them held me fast by the hands, and tied my feet, while the other flogged me severely.

d
We were sold in the usual manner. On a signal given buyers rush at once into the yard where the slaves are held, and make a choice of what they like best. In this manner relations and friends are separated, most of them never to see each other again.

Using a written source

3 Apply the **5×W** rule to **sources c** and **d** to help you answer this question: *How useful are these sources to a historian trying to find out about slavery in the eighteenth century?*

What else do I need to think about?

In order to answer a question like this fully, you will need to think about each of the following.

Bias

A source might be biased. This means that it gives you an argument or an opinion from one person's point of view and is not balanced. But take care. Just because a person may be biased about a particular event or individual, that doesn't mean to say that everything he or she writes or draws is automatically biased too.

Reliability

Once you have checked out the **5×W** rule you will be able to decide whether or not a source tells you accurately about the person, event or time it is describing.

Usefulness

Thinking about the **5×Ws**, **reliability** and **bias** will lead you to consider usefulness (sometimes called utility). When you are thinking about whether a source is useful, you'll need to ask: 'Useful for what?' In this case it is useful as part of an enquiry about slavery.

Remember, every source is useful at some time and for something. Biased sources are useful because they tell you a lot about the person who wrote, drew or painted them. Reliable sources are useful because you can count on them to be telling you accurately about the time, person or event.

Using what you know

4 Apply **bias**, **reliability** and **usefulness** to what Olaudah Equiano had to say about the slavery. You should now have a full answer to the question: *How useful are these sources to a historian trying to find out about slavery in the eighteenth century?*

Communicating about the past

All historians need to be able to be able to communicate their ideas. This can be done in two ways:

- using writing

- verbally.

Whichever way you communicate your ideas, you should do the following.

- **Plan**: map out your work before you start.

- **Structure**: every piece of work should be clearly structured including the use of an introduction and a conclusion.

- **(Use) Evidence**: all ideas should be backed up with accurate information.

The plan

A good plan is the secret to success. It will help you to work out what you want to say before you start.

Your plan should have two parts to it:

- the main points that you are going to make

- what is to be put in each paragraph/section.

You can set out your plan in a number of ways. For example, you might want to use a diagram.

Here is an example plan for the question: *Why did people leave Ireland in the 1840s?*

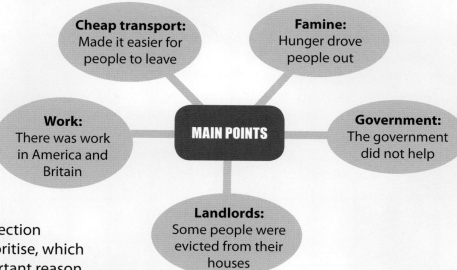

Structure

Think about your paragraph/section running order. You should prioritise, which means putting the most important reason first and the least important reason last.

Introduction: writing out the main points from the plan

1 The most important reason: famine

2 The next most important reason: cheap transport

3 The next most important reason: work elsewhere

4 The next most important reason: landlords

5 The least important reason: the government

Conclusion: sum up your main points

Using evidence

When you make a point, make sure you back it up with evidence. Each paragraph or section should include the following.

- Point: make your point.

- Evidence: back up your point with evidence from sources or your own knowledge.

- Explanation: explain why you have chosen that piece of evidence.

Here is an example of a paragraph.

Evidence	Point	Explanation

The most important reason for people leaving Ireland was the famine. Over 1 million people died between 1845 and 1851 and some areas were without food. As a result people tried to get onto boats that would take them to Britain, America or even New Zealand and Australia where there was plenty of cheap food. In the years of the famine, over 1 million Irish people left Ireland to live abroad.

Put it into practice

5 Why did the Indian Mutiny of 1857 take place?

- What are the main points for your plan?

- What is your paragraph/section running order?

Glossary

Absolute/absolutism
A ruler who has unlimited power.

Annex
When a country gains new land.

Arson
The crime of deliberately starting a fire.

Benefits
This is money given by the state to help people.

Boer
Dutch settlers who lived in Southern Africa.

Ceylon
Small island off the southern tip of India. Now known as Sri Lanka.

Cherokee nation
The collected family of tribes that called themselves 'Cherokee'.

Chickee
A Seminole hut or cabin.

Chieftain
Person in charge of a large Scottish family.

Class
People grouped together socially based on wealth and importance (such as the upper class, the middle class and the poorer or working class).

Colonies
Territories under control of an empire.

Colony
A territory settled or conquered by a people from a distant land.

Community
A group of people who live in a particular area.

Congress
The elected group of politicians responsible for making laws in the USA.

Conscripts
People who are forced to serve in the armed forces.

Constitution
A set of rules that govern Congress.

Croft
The house and land a Scottish family lived on and farmed.

Drill
A regular training routine.

Embers
The still hot, small pieces of wood left over after a fire.

Empire
A collection of territories ruled by one ruler.

Envoy
A special representative who visits a foreign country.

Fetter
Chains around the ankles or wrists.

Fraternity
Friendship and support within a group of people.

Guillotine
An instrument of execution where a sharp blade falls from a frame to cut off a person's head.

Han
The Traditional Chinese people invaded by the Manchus.

Home Secretary
The government minister responsible for the security of the country.

Huguenots
french prostestants from the sixteenth and Seventeenth centuries. They often suffered from oppresion by the Catholic rulers of france.

Imperialism
The desire to expand an empire to increase international power.

Jacobites
The name given to those who believed that James II and his descendants were the rightful Kings of England and Scotland.

Jesuit
A type of Catholic monk.

Landlord
Someone who owns a piece of land.

Lord Protector
Title given to Oliver Cromwell who ruled England from 1653 until his death in 1658.

Lubbers
Term of abuse for an inexperienced sailor.

Manchu
People of the invading country whose leaders became the Qing Emperors.

Manifest destiny
The belief that it was the white settlers' right and purpose in life to settle the lands of America.

Mandarins
Officials in the Chinese civil service.

MP or MPs
An abbreviation for Member of Parliament or Members of Parliament.

Mudlark
Someone who waded in the muddy banks of the River Thames in search of items they could sell, like bits of coal, rope, copper nails and discarded tools. The work was dangerous and dirty, as the water was filthy, and people risked treading on rusty nails and broken glass.

Musket ball
A lead ball fired from a gun.

Mutiny
An uprising against lawful rule.

Native
Term used in Victorian society to describe people in the colonies. It suggests they need to be 'civilised'.

Parliamentarian
Supporter of Parliament in the Civil War. They were also known as 'roundheads' because of their short haircuts.

Paupers
Poor people who received help in the workhouse.

Plantations
Large farms growing sugar or cotton often requiring the use of slave labour.

Poor rate
Payments provided to the poor to help them survive. These payments came from taxes that local people had to pay.

Popery
An old and insulting term for Roman Catholicism.

Preservation
To try to keep something in the condition it was supposed to be in originally.

Punch and Judy shows
Popular puppet show introduced to England in the seventeenth century. Husband and wife, Punch and Judy, were often joined by other characters such as a policeman and a hangman. The puppets were traditionally operated by just one person.

Ragged Schools
Schools set up to teach poor children to read and write for free.

Recruits
People who joined the police force.

Rehabilitating
Helping a prisoner to understand how they could live honestly after they left prison.

Reservation
An area of land set aside for American Indian tribes.

Riot
A public act of violence by a mob.

Riot Act
Act that allowed the local authorities to force a group of twelve or more people to leave a place that they were gathered or face the consequences.

Royalist
Supporters of King Charles. They were also known as cavaliers.

Sabres
Curved swords used by the cavalry.

Scurvy
A disease caused by a lack of vitamin C.

Sepoys
Indian soldiers paid for by the British East India Company.

Shrapnel
Fragments thrown out by an explosion.

Supreme Court
The most powerful court in the United States of America.

Trade winds
These winds, which sweep across the ocean, were relied on by sail ships to complete their journey as quickly as possible.

Transportation
Taking those convicted of crimes to a foreign country as a form of punishment.

Treason
A crime against the government of a country.

Tuberculosis
A lung disease, sometimes known as TB.

US Congress
The American parliament made up of the Senate and the House of Representatives.

Viceroy
British governor of a colony.

Water closet
Outdoor toilet.

Working conditions
What it is like to work in a particular job. This could include pay, tasks and treatment.

Yeomanry
A local volunteer defence force, made up of soldiers on horseback.